From Trust to Terror:

Radical Feminism is Destroying the U.S. Navy

Gerald L. Atkinson

Atkinson Associates Press
6110 Rayburn Drive
Camp Springs, MD 20748

Copyright © 1997 by Gerald L. Atkinson
All rights reserved,
including the right of reproduction
in whole or in part in any form.

Library of Congress Cataloging-in-Publication Data
Atkinson, Gerald L.

From Trust to Terror:
Radical Feminism is Destroying the U.S. Navy

Includes index.
1. Radical Feminism. Modern Liberals   Barbarism.
2. U.S. Navy. Naval aviation training.
3. Destruction of U.S. Military. Affirmative action -- quotas
4. U.S. Navy -- reduced qualification/performance standards
5. U.S. Navy -- Women in combat.

I. Title
VB324.W65Z55   1997
355'.0082 --- dc20   94-45140

ISBN 0-9653277-2-8

Table of Contents

Prologue..i-vi
Introduction..1
Naval Aviation Training..3
The Actors..3
The Author...4
The Student Pilot...4
The Student Pilot's Early History...6
The Student Pilot's Record During Primary Flight Training..................9
The Student Pilot's Record During Advanced Flight Training...............9
The First Progress Review Board for The Student Pilot......................10
    A Surprising Accusation -- Sexual Harassment................................10
    Events leading to the Second Progress Review Board......................12
    The Third Progress Review Board for The Student Pilot..................16
    The Aftermath of the Third Progress Review Board........................18
    Higher Authority's Consideration of the PRB Conclusions...............20
    The Student Pilot's Reclama and Submission of 'Human
    Factors' Reconsideration...21
    The Navy Invokes an Inspector General Investigation.....................22
    The Reporter Tried to 'Do the Right Thing'.....................................25
Trust Turns to Terror in Naval Aviation Training................................28
    Terror in the Ranks of The Flight Instructors..................................29
    Terror at Home, The Relative of a Flight Instructor.......................30
    Terror in the Local 'Free' Press..32
A Summary History of the Reduction of Naval
Aviation Standards...33
    The Tuskegee Airmen..36
    The Case of Ltjg Gary Commock..39
Navy Admits 'Affirmative Action' Policy in Naval
Aviation Training..44
    The Navy's 'Inadvertent' Admission of Reduced
    Standards in Fleet Replacement Squadron Training.........................47
    The Impact of the Navy's 'Affirmative Action' Policy......................49
The Destruction of Naval Aviation...52
    Aviation Safety and Reduced Minimum Standards..........................52
    FNAEBs are the Key to Understanding Reduced
    Minimum Standards..54
    The Fact Of 'Affirmative Action' in Naval Aviation
    Training and the Concomitant Lowering of Minimum
    Standards for All...55
    Even the Famous Blue Angels Are Subject to
    'Affirmative Action'..57
Trust Turned to Terror in the U.S. Navy...58

  The Breakdown of Trust in the U.S. Navy 59
    The Breakdown of Trust at the U.S. Naval Academy 60
    The Mass Media Contribute to the Navy's
    Breakdown of Trust 61
  Terror in the U.S. Navy 64
    Terror in Naval Aviation Training 64
    Terror at the U.S. Naval Academy 66
      The Case of the Mysterious 'Negative Reference 67
    Terror in the U.S. Marine Corps 68
Sensitivity Training: a Tool for Neo-Marxist 'Thought Control' 69
America No Longer 'Understands' Military Service 72
  The Mass Media are Even Less Informed
  of the Military Ethos 75
    The Rebuttal to Evan Thomas' NEWSWEEK Article 76
Technology' is no Crutch for Women-in-Combat 80
  Physical Differences Between Men and Women 80
  Strength, Stamina, and Endurance are Required in
  Combat Aviation 81
  The Move Away from Technology Education at the U.S.
  Naval Academy 88
The Absence of Military Standards in Navy Boot Camp 91
The 'Feminization' of the U.S. Navy Reduces Standards For All 95
Conclusion and Summary 96

Prologue

When the Student Pilot arrived at the naval aviation training base, there was little about her that stood out from her fellow students. True, she was a female student but, while female students are still a minority in naval aviation, there are certainly those who have successfully completed the rigorous flight training program. She was, however, a tall attractive brunette whose sexuality, social immaturity, and obsession with obtaining her Navy 'wings of gold' would not serve her or the U.S. Navy well.

A graduate of the U.S. Naval Academy, she seemed pleasant, dedicated and hard-working. No one knew that she was about to become the most controversial student ever to come through the base -- and one whose actions and influence would either directly or indirectly affect the careers of more than half-a-dozen senior officers. And she would ruin the career of a mid-level Marine officer. In addition, her influence and the 'feminism' which she represented would lead to a **campaign of terror** against tens of junior flight instructors.

After 20 months and a million dollars worth of training, at least five failing grades and a hotly contested ouster from the training program, the Navy finally decided that perhaps The Student Pilot wasn't cut out for naval aviation.

During that time period, The Student Pilot stretched the flexibility of the pilot training program to its utmost -- and strained the tolerance of flight instructors to the limit.

To many disenchanted aviators, she represents 'affirmative action' gone awry. In an attempt to help one lone woman become a fighter pilot, they say, the U.S. Government wasted time and money, endangered the lives of experienced pilots and short-shrifted more deserving male students.

Most importantly, they say, the Navy lowered its standards -- which diminishes the training program, other aviators, and the military's operational readiness.

There are those who may disagree, saying that the male-dominated world of naval aviation is inherently biased against women who must labor twice as hard to get half as far. Others will argue that the Navy's historic lack of minority representation -- particularly in jet aviation -- demands that women and minorities be provided extra opportunities.

All agree that the standard -- the ability to fly a high-performance jet in a 'real' combat environment -- must not be compromised. But by the time The Student Pilot left the base, the resentment she had engendered remained so palpable that few dared speak of her aloud. This is her story.

The Student Pilot immediately set herself apart from her fellow trainees in a series of incidents that involved fraternization. This activity is defined by the Navy as an unduly familiar senior-subordinate relationship, which can erode respect and detract from good order and discipline. Within the training command, students and instructors are prohibited from 'dating.'

The Student Pilot moved in with two male flight instructor pilots -- and had to be told by a commander that this was not allowed. Later on, she went on a cross-country training flight with an instructor and the two shared a hotel room.

Apparently, the training command chose to ignore such incidents, or to disregard them -- because neither brought the student or the instructors any sort of official reprimand.

A second wing commander later tried to excuse The Student Pilot's behavior by saying she was young and didn't know what was expected; however, the Navy routinely and laboriously sends all sailors and aviators through annual training on sexual issues, including fraternization. It is a dubious claim to argue that anyone, much less an officer, is unaware of the Navy's rules about fraternization.

It also became apparent almost immediately that the student was having difficulty with the jet training program. During flight training, instructors grade the students on their performance -- how well they handle the airplane, if they followed proper procedures and whether they meet certain criteria. And they get a grade -- above average, average, below average or unsatisfactory. An 'unsat' is also called a 'down,' and it means that the student failed that part of the training.

If a student receives three downs, he or she faces a Progress Review Board (PRB) to determine if the student should continue training or not. Although students can be attrited (removed from the program) at any time, Navy training instructions list five downs as the maximum number of failing grades a student can receive.

By September -- nine months after her arrival -- Navy officials convened their second progress review board on The Student Pilot's performance. They were trying to decide -- again -- if the student should be ousted from the $1M-per-student training program or allowed to continue.

According to a written summary of the board's findings, The Student Pilot's grades were below average or marginal in familiarization, airways navigation, and radio instruments. After consideration and much debate, Navy officials decided to give the student another chance. But it was not to be her last.

Navy officials say it is unusual for a student to have even one such review board, much less three, during their training tenure. The decision of the board was upsetting for many of the base's male flight instructors, who felt she was receiving far too many chances to finish the program. They wondered among themselves whether a male student would be treated with such leniency.

But even more worrisome for many of them was The Student Pilot's demeanor toward her instructors. She did not take criticism well -- and criticism is a key aspect of the instructional program, where students are debriefed following each flight and told what they could and should do differently and better on the next flight. Instructors said she began to be defensive, or lied about what had occurred on a flight, trying to blame an error on the plane, someone else or the circumstances. At one point, she became hysterical during a debriefing and began crying that 'everyone was out to get her.'

The Student Pilot also quickly gained a reputation for flirting with the male flight instructors, and many witnessed a crucial incident at a 'winging' ceremony -- an incident which would prove to be the key to The Student Pilot's training experience and one which Navy officials took far more seriously than the other two fraternization incidents mentioned above.

The Student Pilot and a senior flight instructor were drinking together at the bar after a 'winging,' as the newly graduated aviators, their families, friends, and classmates celebrated their accomplishments. At some point, The Student Pilot plucked the name tag from the instructor, dropped it down the front of her dress and challenged him to come and get it.

The instructor took the invitation literally, apparently. He and The Student Pilot, accompanied by a third flight instructor, apparently went out drinking a few days later. He and The Student Pilot had planned to rendezvous later, after they had dropped off the other male.

The plan went according to the arrangement, but when the instructor arrived, he and The Student Pilot apparently had a disagreement.

Soon afterward, The Student Pilot approached the other male flight instructor and told him that the first instructor had sexually harassed her. She said she wasn't sure she should file a complaint because she was worried about finishing her flight training.

The instructor said that he was required to report her comments to his superiors -- and he did so. The student and instructor were called before the squadron commanding officer, who questioned both of them about their behavior. It became clear that both the student and the instructor had engaged in **fraternization**. However, when The Student Pilot realized that both would be charged with wrongdoing under a fraternization charge, she retracted her statements -- and got an attorney.

The flight instructor also obtained a lawyer, for his own protection. Navy officials, wary of the unwelcome publicity that a public charge would bring, arranged what was to be a mutually satisfactory agreement -- neither would be charged, the instructor would be transferred and the student could continue flight training.

In fraternization incidents, the U.S. military puts the heaviest blame on the senior partner in the fraternization, reasoning that the more senior participant should behave with more wisdom, seniority, and leadership. But even taking that into account, the command's treatment of the instructor in the fraternization issue is questionable as compared to The Student Pilot's treatment. The instructor pilot was grounded during the investigation process, while The Student Pilot continued flying. The instructor pilot ended up with a non-punitive letter in his file, while the student did not. The instructor pilot was transferred out, while The Student Pilot remained. His career was finished. Her career continued, unblemished.

Soon afterward, The Student Pilot apparently began to feel that flight instructors were hostile toward her or were ostracizing her. Some flight instructors began to speak openly of their reluctance to fly with her -- saying that she shouldn't be allowed in the air.

Privately, they also worried that any failing grade they might give her would turn into a battle cry -- and lead her to charge them with sexual harassment. And no one wanted to take a chance on ruining his career by even a groundless complaint from a female student pilot.

Fellow students found themselves bewildered by the way the female student was being treated. As instructors tried to grade all the students fairly, they began receiving what they felt were conflicting messages from Navy leadership -- to get this female through flight training, no matter what.

As her difficulties with the flight training program continued, the Navy prepared a list of those instructors who could no longer fly with The Student Pilot. Such a list customarily includes all the flight instructors who have previously given the student a down, or failing grade -- the reasoning is that perhaps they will no longer be objective.

In this case, also included on the list were all those flight instructors who had sat on Progress Review Boards to determine if The Student Pilot should continue flight training. And one day, as the list sat on the Scheduling Officer's desk, several flight instructors who were angered by the command's leniency with The Student Pilot, apparently added their names to the list as well.

Soon, The Student Pilot was complaining of being blacklisted by the flight instructors -- and the Wing Commander was enraged. He told flight instructors that if any of them refused to fly with The Student Pilot, they should turn in their wings immediately.

In the aftermath, The Student Pilot asked for and received a transfer from her original squadron to a sister squadron, where Navy officials hoped she would be able to start anew. She began flying in the new squadron, working diligently but still struggling as she slowly progressed through the flying syllabus.

Few faulted her motivation. She was reportedly dedicated and intelligent, often showing up in the ready room before dawn to gain extra flying time in an empty back seat. She studied hard and was well prepared for each flight.

The Student Pilot impressed her flight instructors frequently with her abilities to fly smoothly, staying ahead of the aircraft; know and demonstrate procedures, and fly formation. However, her performance was inconsistent. She lined up on the wrong runway; came in too fast and too close to another plane on a weapons detachment in El Centro, CA; and failed to follow proper procedure for visually identifying her fellow training planes during a three-plane dogfight exercise.

She had trouble with landings, instrument scanning, and -- perhaps most significantly -- situational awareness. One Progress Review Board reported their concerns with her decision-making ability and her tendency to become overwhelmed with data. "*Must have SA (situational awareness) and use it to make good decisions. She seems to be overloaded with input when she becomes task saturated, and makes bad decisions -- both in the air and on the ground preparing for flights,*" wrote one Navy official.

The Chief of Naval Air Training (CNATRA), who later reviewed The Student Pilot's records during an investigation into her case, decided that she was clearly getting the benefit of the doubt. "*While she has many flights with good (above average) performance, she has an equivalent number of below average flights. Upon closer scrutiny, it is evident to me that she performs well when the flight is progressing well, but does very badly when the flight does not proceed as planned or as desired. The five flights that were graded 'unsatisfactory' have a common denominator: unsafe flight performance related either to lack of situational awareness or poor headwork,*" he wrote.

"*There is no doubt that [she] strongly desires to receive her 'wings of gold.' That desire and enthusiasm have served her well and seem to ensure her excellent preparation for every flight. It does not, however, guarantee her performance at any flight. Failure to consistently perform at an acceptable level is the problem in this case and is well documented. In fact, my review of her training record revealed at least two additional flights [the second FAM-19 and both WEP-8Xs] which could justifiably have been graded 'unsatisfactory' and were not. She was clearly getting the benefit of the doubt,"* CNATRA added.

As The Student Pilot's training progressed shakily, the flight instructors reached a crisis point. Concerned about the way her training was progressing and the leniency with which she was being treated, they came forward to their superiors-- and were dismissed. They gave her failing grades, and the grades were overturned by higher authority. Finally, some decided to talk to the media about The Student Pilot -- in hopes of shedding some light on the dark dealings of the Navy's commanding officers.

The flight instructors spoke off the record of their concerns and tried to provide a reporter with information to back up their comments. The reporter, in turn, sought to interview other flight instructors so as to verify the comments and story. Many Navy officials, including some flight instructors and students, confirmed the story. Others declined to talk, worried about their careers and the wrath of their commanders.

After gathering information about the case, the reporter attempted to interview The Student Pilot for her side of the story -- and was turned away. The reporter also attempted to interview Navy leaders about the case -- and they, too, chose not to speak on the record about the case. They would, however, speak 'off-the-record.' No one was willing to go public with the details and the frustrated reporter was eventually forced to abandon the story.

Finally, The Student Pilot, who was one of four female students at the base at the time, was attrited from the program -- 20 months after she began. She appealed the decision twice, but it was finally upheld. The Wing Commander tried to help her obtain a transfer to another aviation community, but that too was rejected. The Student Pilot remains in the Navy, but is no longer in naval aviation. The official reason for her removal is failure of flight performance, a catchall term that basically say The Student Pilot 'didn't have the right stuff.'

Some flight instructors, relieved that the Navy finally attrited The Student Pilot, want to let the matter die. Others say that there may be more students like her -- and that the command should have been more assertive in ousting her as soon as she flaunted the rules regarding fraternization and performed poorly in the air.

This case has inflamed Navy pilots' worst fears about women-in-combat; that they don't fit in, that they'll get breaks, that they're not as good as their male counterparts and that political pressure will weaken naval aviation -- and thereby diminish readiness and endanger the nation's military pilots.

There were many transgressions committed during The Student Pilot's training tenure -- by The Student Pilot, by flight instructors who fraternized with her, by the commanding officers who failed to maintain the Navy's good order and discipline, professionalism and high standards for the rigorous profession that is naval aviation.

A squadron Commanding Officer left under a cloud during her tenure, reprimanded by his commander for failing to maintain discipline and professionalism among his flight instructors. A Wing Commander who failed to properly handle the fraternization incident resigned (retired). The second Wing Commander, who tried to repair the damage done and ended up giving The Student Pilot even more chances -- thereby angering the flight instructors even more -- also resigned (retired) after receiving a poor evaluation over his handling of the case.

Even more troubling is the activity that injected **terror** into the lives of the young male flight instructors who tried to 'do the right thing.' They were intimidated, threatened with dismissal, and forced to undergo Inspector General investigations or were threatened with such investigations if they did not cooperate with their commanders' desires to 'pass' The Student Pilot, <u>no matter what</u>. They were forced to seek legal counsel in order to protect themselves from the destructive intimidation invoked by their superiors. The injection of **terror** into the lives of these flight instructors is the new dimension of totalitarianism, driven by a political agenda, that is destroying naval aviation. The details of this story are provided in this book.

Meanwhile, brave young 'warriors' are being lost to naval aviation. Impossible to count are the Navy flight instructor pilots who chose (and are now choosing) to quit naval aviation and are now flying for the commercial airlines -- leaving their much loved profession in disgust over the Navy's handling of this case. It is their loss that the Navy -- and this nation -- should mourn.

Introduction

This is a story of intimidation and terror. It occurred in a premiere component of our nation's military -- the U.S. Navy. The dagger of fear has been plunged into the hearts of young naval officers who would 'do the right thing.'

Americans who follow the national debate on women-in-combat have been led to believe that this experiment involves a logical choice: the rational balancing of 'equal opportunity' for women in the military and military readiness. But this exercise in logic does not capture the truth about the experiment. Under the guise of 'equal opportunity' for women, young men in the Navy are being **terrorized** by a totalitarian regimen of intimidation. This totalitarianism employs **terror** to achieve its goal, which is a 'feminized' Navy where <u>career advancement</u> for females supersedes all other considerations -- even at the cost of plummeting morale, professional performance, and combat readiness. As a result, the Navy's 'warriors' are leaving the service.

A destructive trend has surfaced in the wake of all of this. That is the **loss of trust**. Mutual **trust** is the foundation, the glue that binds all who subject themselves to high risk in dangerous, hazardous professional environments such as carrier naval aviation. In over 22 years of naval aviation service, I have never found a fellow naval aviator who I could not trust with my life, whether he be a flight instructor, division leader, section leader, catapult officer, landing signal officer, or commanding officer. Mutual trust and respect comes from the knowledge that no one could progress through the demanding qualification and training process of naval aviation who did not pass the **personal** and **professional scrutiny** of a flight instructor or other '<u>protector of the trust</u>.'

Before the advent of 'affirmative action,' flight instructors had the dominant input to decisions of 'who stays' and 'who goes.' Before the advent of 'affirmative action,' every naval aviator could look every other naval aviator in the eye and know that each had passed these tests. The tests were <u>eminently professional</u>, and they were <u>very personal</u>. Mutual **trust** was everywhere. Now, in the advent of 'affirmative action,' and especially its invocation for women-in-combat, **that trust is being destroyed**.

This episode illustrates a **complete breakdown of trust**. Trust has been broken between high-ranking officers and the warriors whose fate it is to fight the battles into which these officers send them. Trust has been broken between mid-level officer commissars who are riding the wave of 'affirmative action' policy to enhance their careers and these same warriors. Trust has been broken between instructor pilots (the warriors) and some of their students who are not aeronautically qualified, except by reduced standards which superiors force upon these instructors in advancing substandard students. And finally, trust has been broken between aviators who meet traditionally high standards and those substandard 'affirmative action' aviators who achieve their wings as a result of special consideration, repeated remedial training, and finally the resultant reduced standards in aviation training and qualification.

So, this is a story of 'affirmative action' programs gone awry, the implementation of a totalitarian political control over a traditionally 'democratic' military structure that is deeply rooted in the American people and in American democracy. The U.S. military defends our constitution and serves as the guarantor of the American experiment with democracy from external and internal threats. It does not serve the ends of a totalitarian state. Yet, a component of that military, the U.S. Navy, is disintegrating under totalitarian activities motivated, encouraged, and approved by the very government which it serves.

On a smaller scale, this is a story of the U.S. Navy cover-up of fraternization between a failed female student pilot and her flight instructors -- in which the female ruined the careers of at least two instructor pilots while receiving nary a reprimand from naval authorities. This is a story of the seeds that have been planted which are leading to the chaotic disintegration of one of the nation's finest institutions. Radical feminism is destroying the U.S. Navy.

This story is a part of a larger story now being repeated for the U.S. Army in its initial stages of 'sexual harassment' scandals at Aberdeen Proving Ground, MD, Fort Jackson, SC, and other training sites for our nation's soldiers. The pattern that emerged after the Navy's notorious Tailhook '91 'scandal' is being repeated with the U.S. Army. The same subversive forces that were at work to destroy the U.S. Navy are now busy laying the groundwork for destruction of the U.S. Army. The pattern is exactly the same.

The 'warriors' are being separated from their high-level leadership. A barrier is being constructed between those who fight America's wars and those who send them to their fate. Radical feminists[1] and their allies in the Clinton administration, Congress, and the media who have destroyed the morale of the U.S. Navy are carrying out the same campaign against the U.S. Army. Both campaigns have taken advantage of allegations of 'scandalous' sexual harassment arising out of the natural tensions between men and women placed in close contact by the fact of women-in-the-military, a long-standing goal of the radical feminists.

Reduced training and qualification standards are part of but are not the most important element of this story. These standards have been gradually but perceptibly reduced over the past fifteen years[2] in the U.S. Navy. The impact of this reduction is just now being revealed. Gradually and almost imperceptibly over the years, 'affirmative action' programs have been introduced into naval aviation training and officer training in the U.S. Navy. These programs have led to reduced **minimum** standards across the board -- from the selection of the Chief of Naval Operations to the 'winging[3]' of naval aviators, to the commissioning of officers at the U.S. Naval Academy.

---

[1] Bork, Robert H., "Slouching Towards Gomorrah: Modern Liberalism and American Decline," Regan Books (HarperCollins), 1996. Judge Bork describes a 'modern liberalism' with roots in the radical Sixties which is characterized by a 'totalitarian spirit.' He identifies 'radical feminists' as the most dominant element in this movement. He concludes that these 'barbarians' are at the heart of the present 'American decline.'

[2] First detailed in a book by Gerald L. Atkinson, 'The New Totalitarians: Bosnia as a Mirror of America's Future,' Atkinson Associates Press, P.O. Box 1417, Clinton, MD 20735, 1996.

[3] A 'winging' is a formal Navy celebration of the graduation of naval aviation candidates who have earned their coveted 'wings of gold.' All graduates, flight instructors, and their wives, relatives, fiancées, and girl friends dress in their finest formal attire and enjoy an evening of boisterous fun at the Officers' Club with the aid of ample quantities of alcoholic beverages.

The new and most damaging element in all of this is the **reign of terror** being imposed on those within the Navy who try to maintain at least the minimum standards. They know from experience in fleet squadrons under severe operating circumstances -- at night, on stormy seas, in all-weather conditions -- that fleet aviators' lives become endangered by 'winging' substandard naval aviation candidates. This new element of terror has coincided with the radical feminists' political initiative to open combat roles to women -- purely for career enhancing reasons. To them career 'opportunity' trumps military effectiveness. In reality, their goal is the raw use of power, to exert their will on an institution, the U.S. Navy, which has been from its inception male-oriented.

This **reign of terror** is being conducted by mid-level naval officers acting under the cover of high-ranking flag officers who are imposing a radical feminist agenda on the Navy at the behest of their civilian superiors. Both the Clinton administration and the Congress are equally to blame as the principal cause of this reign of terror. They are acceding to and, indeed, carrying out a radical feminist agenda designed by special interest groups aimed at the destruction of the U.S. armed forces. They are accomplishing this with the direct complicity of the U.S. media -- television, newsprint, and radio. They are accomplishing this while **the American people sleep**!

Naval Aviation Training

To understand this story, you must know a little about naval aviation training. The process of becoming a Navy pilot begins with Aviation Preflight Indoctrination, a six-week ground school at Naval Air Station Pensacola, FL. Students then are assigned to primary flight training at NAS Pensacola or NAS Corpus Christi, TX.

Training consists of both academics and flying, with students receiving frequent evaluation and scrutiny by the instructors. After 22 to 26 weeks of primary training, students are sorted into pipelines or career tracks. The top students generally get to choose their assignments, and most choose jets. Other choices include maritime, or propeller planes; helicopters; and E2/C2s, an electronic surveillance aircraft (or a carrier cargo version).

Students assigned to jet training then go to NAS Kingsville, TX or NAS Meridian, MS, where they train for about 10 months before receiving their Navy 'wings of gold.' The competition continues -- top graduates in the jet program get their choice of aircraft in the fleet, with most opting for the fastest fighter jets, such as the F-14 Tomcat and the F/A-18 Hornet. They undergo training in these aircraft in a Fleet Replacement Squadron (FRS). Students assigned to fly helicopters and propeller planes continue at NAS Corpus Christi, or go to NAS Pensacola or Whiting Field in Milton, FL.

The Actors

The story told here is true. All of the events recorded here have actually occurred and real live people have participated in them. The story must be told, however, in a 'fictional' format in order to protect the privacy of the individuals involved. Consequently, instead of actual names, a category of individual will speak for each real life individual. The category may be a composite sketch of several actual individuals. These 'Actors' are: The Author (me), The Student Pilot, The Flight Instructor(s), The Flight Surgeon(s), The Relative, The Wing Commander, CNATRA (Chief of Naval Air Training), The Newspaper and The Lawyers. The story is told from the perspective of these Actors.

The Author

The Author is a retired U.S. Navy carrier aviator with fighter, attack (including nuclear weapons delivery), and reconnaissance aircraft experience. He has deployed on four extended carrier cruises with one combat cruise in Vietnam. He was a U.S. Navy test pilot and landing signal officer. He flight-demonstrated the RA5C 'Vigilante' in the 1965 Paris Air Show. The Author knows something of the concept of a naval officer and carrier aviator and the mental and emotional rigors of being shot at and his aircraft hit by a determined enemy intent on killing him.

The Author understands at the gut and intellectual levels the bond that exists among 'warriors' who trust each other to 'do the right thing' in mortal combat. One element of that trust is to 'tell the truth' regardless of personal consequences. Another important element of this trust is knowing that your 'warrior' squadron-mates had to pass the same rigorous, stringent, and demanding standards of qualification that you passed. The Author knows from practical experience that Navy flight instructors are the guarantors of that trust which is the backbone of naval aviation. These flight instructors are seasoned naval aviators who have experienced at least one tour of sea duty in an operational squadron. Traditionally, only those who pass the test of rigorous training and qualification standards are allowed through the gate to wear the coveted Navy 'wings of gold.'

The Author was awarded the Legion of Merit, the Distinguished Flying Cross, the Air medal with four stars, and a few others not worth mentioning (the latter, some of the same medals that ADM Jeremy Boorda allegedly committed suicide over) during his 'warrior' service in the U.S. Navy during the Cold War.

The Author's attention was brought to this story by at least two patriotic Americans who became aware of gross inequities in the qualification standards for training naval aviators at one of the U.S. Navy's premier training bases. They were also aware of the rising morale problem that this situation was creating due to a complete breakdown of trust. One of these loyal Americans is a former Vietnam Prisoner of War (POW) and the other is a close family relative of a former flight instructor at the air base. Their interest inspired contact with many naval aviators, active duty and inactive reserves who made themselves known to The Author, and who supplied, corroborated and added details of which you are about to learn.

The Student Pilot

A principal character in this story is a failed student pilot, a female, who was accorded unprecedented and extraordinary consideration in her attempt to meet the minimum qualification and training standards for earning her Navy 'wings of gold.' But that is not the heart of the story. The real story is one of **intimidation** and **threats to the careers** of courageous instructor pilots who attempted to 'do the right thing' by maintaining minimum standards in spite of the **campaign of terror** instituted by the 'affirmative action' milicrats at the mid-level chain of command and their civilian radical feminist allies, The Lawyers.

The story has been completely covered up by the U.S. Navy for fear of exposure of a poisonous swamp within naval aviation training. Indeed, this poison pervades the entire U.S. Navy but it has revealed itself in a particularly harmful way at this training base. It is important that this story is revealed to the American people because it is a harbinger of what is to come for the entire U.S. military establishment -- its complete and utter destruction.

Radical feminist organizations and the national mass media are attempting to emasculate the U.S. Army by taking advantage of the 'scandals' at the Aberdeen Proving Ground to reach the same state of affairs as is revealed in this story for the U.S. Navy. Six years after the Navy's Tailhook '91 sexual harassment 'scandal' the pattern is repeating itself -- now with the U.S. Army. That state of affairs is the implementation of a **campaign of terror** to intimidate those who would 'tell the truth' about what is really going on inside the U.S. military.

This same pattern will emerge for the U.S. Air Force in the aftermath of the LT Kelly Flinn affair. After committing adultery with the husband of an enlisted airman at her B-52 base and engaging in sexual fraternization with another enlisted man, she lied about her adultery and disobeyed a direct order to 'cease and desist' such activities. LT Flinn's pending court martial was cancelled and she was granted a general discharge under honorable conditions. The first female Secretary of the Air Force, Sheila E. Widnall, granted this unheard-of dispensation to the first female B-52 pilot after LT Flinn's parents hired a publicist and a masterful lawyer to propagandize American public opinion through a ready and willing television and print media[4]. The result of this brouhaha will be extreme feminist political pressure on high-ranking Air Force officers to imitate the same cowardice shown by their Navy counterparts in the wake of Tailhook '91. Just watch the headlines of major national newspapers. The U.S. Air Force and the U.S. Army will be taken down the same path that is destroying the U.S. Navy.

The common link between this Navy story and the emerging Air Force and Army stories is the double standard for disciplining males and females in today's feminized military. The Student Pilot in this story got away with two major incidents of 'fraternization' with her flight instructors without a single charge being filed against her. The flight instructors, one married, were cashiered -- their careers ruined under the cover of administrative action by the Navy. This double standard cannot continue. If it does, the **breakdown of trust** will be complete.

The Student Pilot is a female graduate of the U.S. Naval Academy who failed to earn her 'wings' at one of the Navy's flight training bases. She was a substandard student pilot who had a history of using her sexuality and 'threat of discrimination' charges to cover for her incompetent flying performance. She was definitely not 'naval aviation material.' But due to the 'affirmative action' atmosphere in the U.S. Navy at large and at this training base in particular, she simply could not be attrited[5] in spite of substandard performance as a student aviator without a high-level (possibly CNO-level) <u>political decision</u>.

The Student Pilot was subjected to three Progress Review Boards (PRBs), evaluation boards convened to ascertain the reasons for substandard flying proficiency, before finally being attrited. At the time of the last PRB,

---

[4] Vistica, Gregory L., and Thomas, Evan, "Sex and Lies," NEWSWEEK, pp. 26, 2 June 1997.

[5] A naval aviation candidate is 'attrited,' that is, 'washed out' or dismissed from flight training when it is apparent that, for one reason or another, he or she is not considered aeronautically adapted for flying. The candidate has failed to meet naval aviation requirements and is dropped from the program.

she had accumulated five formally recorded 'downs[6],' including three in Phase I (two in FAM Stage), and up to four additional 'excused downs.' Although a naval aviation candidate can be removed from flight training with as few as one or two failed flights, Navy guidelines state that the wing commander must obtain permission from the Chief of Naval Air Training (CNATRA) to retain a student who has received five 'downs.'

The Student Pilot was definitely not aeronautically adapted for flying. But, given the 'affirmative action' climate in today's Navy, it became nearly impossible to attrit her. Instead, she nearly ruined the career of at least one instructor pilot who was completely innocent of any wrongdoing but who was **scapegoated and terrorized** by The Wing Commander who championed The Student Pilot's cause to win her wings in spite of her clearly demonstrated insufficient flying qualities.

The Student Pilot's story is well known at the training base. Many people there are knowledgeable of the details. They include other student pilots (male and female), those who flew with The Student Pilot, those who had professional discussions with The Student Pilot, and those who have had discussions with those who flew with The Student Pilot. If these people could be interviewed, the truth would be easily and quickly verified. Unfortunately, the identification of those who know the truth would result in their summary dismissal and/or career termination with the U.S. Navy. Some of these people are married and have young children to support. Nevertheless, if they stand on principle and tell the truth, their careers are abruptly terminated. No hearing. No chance to reclama. Dead in the water. Done! Such is the **reign of terror** which is so pervasive in the current U.S. Navy at all levels as well as at this training base.

The details of this story could be verified independently by conducting extensive interviews with each of the individual actors, many of whom have now scattered to the far corners of the earth with orders to other duty stations, retirement, and resignation. The story was not published at the time of the occurrence of the events, however, because of the extension of the **reign of terror** into the civilian realm -- against The Newspaper. But I am getting ahead of the story.

The Student Pilot's Early History

The Student Pilot, although apparently a central figure in this story, is actually a pawn. She is a female who has been used by those forces within and outside the U.S. Navy, the radical feminists, to advance an 'affirmative action' agenda which has gone terribly awry. This is an agenda which is destroying naval aviation and which, if unchecked, will completely destroy the entire U.S. military.

While a midshipman at the Naval Academy, The Student Pilot was enrolled in the local flying program, learning to fly light propeller-driven civilian airplanes. During a solo flight she landed and went off the runway, wrecking the aircraft. According to her classmates, she was absolved of fault and her instructor was blamed for her accident. He was faulted for

---

[6] A 'down' is a term used to describe a training flight wherein the student fails to perform the required flying tasks in a satisfactory manner. It is a failed flight in which the student may be either dangerous, unsafe, or just plain incompetent in performing the flight task. Any failed flight must be re-flown in order to pass on to the next flight in a sequence of training flights. Instructor pilots are professionals who are trained to ascertain and have experience in ascertaining the level of competence demonstrated by the student.

failing to provide adequate training in cross-wind landings before allowing her to solo. Her classmates say that cross-wind was not a factor in the mishap. Furthermore, she was returning to the field after sunset (a 'pinky' night landing), which was not authorized for solo students. Most of her Naval Academy classmates know of this story. It is indicative of the trouble that was to follow.

The Student Pilot is a U.S. Naval Academy graduate with a current rank of Ltjg. She is a hard-working, conscientious, and highly motivated individual who has been observed putting in many extra hours in preparation for each scheduled training flight. She would undoubtedly be a well-qualified naval officer but is simply not aeronautically adapted to the flying profession. If anything, it has been observed that The Student Pilot 'over-prepared' for each flight in the sense that, if unanticipated events occurred, she could not adapt to the changed conditions. If all did not go as planned, she was lost. Nevertheless, her spirit and determination have been commended by those who know her.

What The Student Pilot does not have, however, is the set of mental and physical skills that render her naval aviation qualified. Many very capable naval officers are not sufficiently aeronautically adapted to become naval aviators. Her determination to succeed, however, <u>turned into an obsession</u> which was indulged by the U.S. Navy climate of 'extreme reconsideration of individual performance weaknesses' that now has become standard[7,8,9,10] in naval aviation -- that is, the lowering of traditional qualification standards. This climate exists in spades at the training base in this story.

The Student Pilot has been characterized by some as 'immature'[11] in her social relationships. She has been observed in a drunken state at parties

---

[7] Atkinson, Gerald L., 'The New Totalitarians: Bosnia as a Mirror of America's Future,' Atkinson Associates Press, P.O. Box 1417, Clinton, MD 20735, 1996.

[8] For example, see Scarborough, Rowan, "Navy says female pilots got extra help," The Washington Times, 24 February 1997, for an official Navy report that admits (now three years after the fact) that LT Carey Dunai Lohrenz (who since has been removed from combat aviation for safety-of-flight reasons) received *'unprecedented and unusual aid...'* in her F-14A combat training when she and LT Kara Hultgreen (who also received *'special consideration'* in her training and died as a result of it) undertook training to become combat aviators.

[9] Caldwell, Robert J., "Navy admits 'concessions' for female F-14 pilots: Internal report sheds new light on charges of training bias," The San Diego Union-Tribune, 2 March 1997.

[10] For example, see Boyer, Peter J., "What Killed Admiral Boorda: Admiral Boorda's War," The New Yorker, pp. 68, 16 September 1996, for a description of a failed helicopter trainee, LT Rebecca Hansen, whose obsession with completing flight training in spite of her demonstrated inadequate flight performance resulted in the 'firing' of ADM Stanley Arthur, a Vietnam and Gulf Storm war hero, after he correctly concurred in flight instructors' judgements that she should be attrited -- 'washed out' of flight training.

[11] Single quote marks are used throughout this book to indicate a direct quote from one or more of The Actors in this story. These real life persons must remain anonymous because of their abject fear of being identified. Such is the breadth and depth of the **reign of terror** invoked by authorities in this story. These actors fear that they and/or their loved ones will be pursued and lose their jobs, or worse, if identified. They live daily in fear (can you imagine this in the United States of

in which both students and flight instructors and their wives were in attendance. She has been observed 'throwing herself' at male officers, including flight instructors, at these parties. This 'immaturity' may stem from a troubled family life which is known but will not be discussed here.

When The Student Pilot was a sophomore at the Naval Academy, she dated a senior. They had problems. She reported to authorities that he had beaten her up about two weeks before his graduation. As a result of his actions, the senior midshipman was kicked out of the Naval Academy just before he was to graduate.

Later on, it is rumored that she claimed a midshipman got her pregnant. An investigation was conducted. The charge turned out to be untrue. It was determined that she had made a 'false official statement.' An 'honor board' was convened to address this determination. The 'honor board' took no action on her false charge. This occurred in spite of the fact that making a 'false official statement' is a violation of the Uniform Code of Military Justice. Rumor has it that she gave her 'big-eyed puppy routine and cried' and they let her off. Those who have observed, first hand, her behavior during Progress Review Boards conducted later on at the naval aviation training base claim that she is a master at this tactic. A female naval Flight Surgeon has attested to observing this behavior.

After being commissioned as an Ensign, The Student Pilot and three others were stashed away at Patuxent River, MD to await orders to Basic Flight Training. Another newly commissioned Ensign in their class was 'stashed away' in his home town recruiting office awaiting orders to commence flight training. As the time for him to report to primary flight training approached, his grandmother took ill (she was not expected to live beyond two weeks). This officer called the Student Control Officer at NAS Pensacola and requested a three-week delay. The delay was denied and he reported to primary flight training on time.

Later on, this male officer discovered that The Student Pilot had been given a three-month extension at the request of a Commander with whom she was 'involved' while 'stashed away' at NAS Patuxent River. The three other newly commissioned male Ensigns who were also 'stashed away' at Pax River with The Student Pilot were friends of the male Ensign who had been denied an extension to be with his sick relative. Although these Ensigns had no proof that the Commander and The Student Pilot were 'sleeping together,' there was a strong perception that this was the case. They knew, however, that the Commander personally flew to NAS Pensacola to request the three-month delay for The Student Pilot. The Student Control Officer there initially denied her request which led to a heated discussion between the the Commander and the Student Control Officer. The level of their argument became so loud that people in the outer office could overhear the discussion. The Student Pilot's request for a three-month extension was finally granted. The seeds of a pattern of 'preference' appeared to be forming -- special favors for a member of a 'protected' group, women, in naval aviation training.

America) of such identification. One exception to this rule of single-quote-marks is the phrase, 'affirmative action.' This phrase is single-quoted to denote the entire aura that has arisen with this term and its political, higher education, workplace, and legal depths in American culture. Double quote marks are reserved for quotations from newspapers, television, or private conversations with those who are not vulnerable to the **reign of terror** described herein.

The Student Pilot's Record During Primary Flight Training

It is rumored that while The Student Pilot was at Whiting Field, FL (one of the Navy's primary flight training bases), she became romantically involved with a flight instructor, a Marine Captain. Other naval aviation candidates at Whiting at the time have said that the instructor pilot 'magically' disappeared when this 'fraternization' relationship became known to Navy authorities. The Student Pilot was not disciplined for her part in the affair.

This behind-the-scenes administrative cover-up of an activity that is a violation of the Uniform Code of Military Justice accomplishes two things. Presumably, the flight instructor gets off lightly with a reassignment without a disciplinary infraction on his record while the female has her reputation restored. In reality, this kind of activity simply relieves the supervisory naval authorities from the public scrutiny and/or visibility to their superior officers in the chain of command. A public and/or official Navy airing would bring nothing but 'trouble' for their own careers. Far worse, this activity creates an unintended consequence, that is, a climate in which the double standard of discipline for females and males undermines morale and breaks down trust.

At Whiting, it was widely rumored that The Student Pilot received 'below average' flight grades. The flight instructors there have told others that they were forced to inflate her grades to 'beef up' her apparent performance. Thus, members of a protected (quotaed) group were routinely given inflated grades to assure the 'success' of that 'affirmative action' group -- in this case, women.

Some of The Flight Instructors at the naval air training base which is the subject of this story saw her primary training record, which was available for review, as it is in all PRBs. They did not notice anything 'out of the ordinary' but caution that at the time of her early PRBs, stories of her past training experience had not yet reached the advanced aviation training base.

The Student Pilot's Record During Advanced Flight Training

Shortly after The Student Pilot arrived at the Navy base on 16 November 1994 for advanced flight training, she started exhibiting social behavior that clearly 'crossed the line' of propriety for a naval officer. She regularly attended 'wingings' and other social functions, became inebriated, and flirted with instructor pilots (IPs). During these social occasions, her behavior became so noticeable that some flight instructors, their wives, and male student pilots were starting to complain.

As time went on, The Student Pilot began to focus primarily on her training squadron's Operations Officer, a Marine Captain. At a party at the Officer's Club, The Student Pilot was observed inebriated while playfully taking this IP's name tag off his uniform and placing it down her bra and taunting "*If you want it, go get it.*"

Over time, this IP became carried away and agreed to a romantic liaison with The Student Pilot, suggested and arranged by her. But the IP 'chickened out' and did not follow through. He later admitted this entire occasion of public flirtation to his wife, explaining that he had 'gotten carried away and made a fool of himself.' But the incident did not stop there with The Student Pilot. More on that later.

The First Progress Review Board for The Student Pilot

At about the same time as the 'fraternization' incident described above, The Student Pilot encountered flying problems during flight familiarization (FAM) stage. She received two 'downs' during FAM stage:

- The <u>first</u> failed training flight, or 'down,' was awarded The Student Pilot on 17 April '95 during a Fam-14x for poor procedures. This 'down' was earned during a 'safe-for-solo' check ride. The Student Pilot did not correctly utilize or interpret the output of an electronic guide to proper flight performance.

After this 'down,' The Student Pilot was given two ETs (Extra Training flights) and then a recheck. The IP who gave the recheck returned from the flight and told the squadron commander 'I've got to give her a down.' After the flight, he had sought advice from three or four other flight instructors and they agreed that her deviations from competent flying performance during the IP's check ride were sufficient to give her a 'down.' The reason that the IP discussed this flight with other instructor pilots was that he wanted a 'quality assurance' on his decision to give her a 'down' on a recheck. Although it has happened in the past, it is rare for a student to fail a recheck.

The IP then went to the squadron commander to tell him of his conclusion. The CO **directed** that the IP 'give her an incomplete.' The 'reason' for the 'incomplete' was *weather conditions*, which was one of the IP's concerns when he went to talk with other IPs. Thus, the first of a series of 'excused downs' was awarded The Student Pilot.

- The <u>second</u> 'down' was given on 30 April '95 during an R1-9 flight for a poor approach. This 'down' was awarded by her training squadron Executive Officer on a cross-country flight to Patuxent River, MD. This very experienced flight instructor was a former Navy Test Pilot and Test Pilot Instructor, while previously stationed at NAS Patuxent River. The Student Pilot turned the wrong way, outbound instead of inbound from the navigation aid to the landing field.

As a result of these two 'downs', a Progress Review Board was convened for The Student Pilot. Little is known of this PRB other than the fact of its occurrence. As is the case with most 'first' PRBs, attempts were most likely made to ascertain the reasons for The Student Pilot's substandard flying performance. This normally is accomplished in a positive sympathetic atmosphere which gives the fledgling aviator the benefit of every doubt. This is especially the practice whenever a student appears to be slow in assimilating the flight instruction but has not demonstrated dangerous tendencies. The Student Pilot was given a favorable recommendation to continue flight training.

A Surprising Accusation -- Sexual Harassment

Shortly after The Student Pilot's first PRB, she confided to the Student Control Officer (who was also her class advisor) that *'After I graduate from the program, I am going to bring fraternization charges against [the marine Captain flight instructor described above, the Operations Officer].'* The Student Control Officer told her that any such charge would have to be investigated immediately. The Student Control Officer told her that, given what she had just told him, he had no choice but to inform the training squadron's Commanding Officer.

Over the next few days the Commanding Officer (CO) interviewed The Student Pilot and the Operations Officer. The Student Pilot insisted that fraternization was indeed going on between them. The CO then called for a preliminary investigation (PI) on the charge of fraternization. A PI is an <u>informal</u> local investigation which is often called by a commanding officer to ascertain the facts in a local dispute within the command which could affect morale or good order and discipline. The PI, conducted by Training Wing personnel (two Lieutenants -- O-3s), determined that the facts of the case definitely constituted fraternization between The Student Pilot and the Operations Officer.

The CO then told The Student Pilot that if fraternization indeed had occurred, both she and the Operations Officer would be in trouble. Hearing that she was now in jeopardy of disciplinary action, she then changed her story and told the CO that she meant 'sexual harassment,' not fraternization. Subsequently, the CO had a second PI convened to investigate a charge of sexual harassment of The Student Pilot by the Operations Officer. This PI, conducted by the same two LTs, found that there was no sexual harassment in the relationship between The Student Pilot and the Operations Officer.

After all was said and done, the Commanding Officer briefed all instructor pilots in the squadron at an all-instructors-meeting during which the results of the two PIs were disseminated. Both of the investigating officers had conducted a fair and impartial investigation. Fraternization was confirmed; sexual harassment was excluded.

The written results of both preliminary investigations, at one time, resided in the Commanding Officer's office but are probably unknown to the current squadron Commanding Officer. A secretary has been observed taking the complete package of the written PIs out of the CO's desk, but no flight instructor has seen it. Still, it exists or at least it existed at the time during which The Student Pilot was at the advanced training base.

Thus, the investigations, conducted within the training squadron, revealed that the sexual harassment charges were, indeed, not sexual harassment but implicated both the Operations Officer and The Student Pilot in a 'fraternization' relationship which is a violation of Navy regulations. At this point, The Student Pilot retained the service of two lawyers in the informal investigation. The Student Pilot (accompanied by two lawyers) <u>maintained her accusation</u> of <u>sexual harassment</u> against the IP, in spite of solid evidence of fraternization. Obviously the 'fraternization' charge would implicate The Student Pilot as well as the IP, requiring equal or at least some measure of punishment for her.

The Lawyers insisted that the two previous 'downs' awarded The Student Pilot be 'excused,' that is, wiped from the record in consideration of the stress that the 'sexual harassment' incident had placed on her. For them, the trauma of 'sexual harassment' was the cause of The Student Pilot's poor flying performance. They wanted The Student Pilot to be given a 'clean slate' -- a chance to start anew. The Navy commanders obviously could not openly agree to such a grave violation of training standards.

The deadlock was broken by the parties entering into an informal agreement that would cause 'the least harm' to all concerned. Little did they know that this cozy little agreement would foment extreme unrest in the naval aviation community at the base.

The result of this informal agreement was that the 'guilty' IP magically 'disappeared,' that is, given orders to another geographic location. This is the second time during The Student Pilot's flight training that this pattern had occurred. She completely evaded any punishment for a violation of Navy regulations for which she was at least as, or more than, equally responsible.

None of this is recorded in any <u>official</u> report. The whole affair has been purposely 'hushed up' at the training base. Again, all concerned (except the unfortunate Marine Captain[12] and his wife) were protected by the cloak of secrecy surrounding this episode. The Student Pilot, the squadron Commanding Officer, The Wing Commander, and all superiors up the chain of command were now protected from any fallout. All of these actors must have been quite relieved that the media would not get wind of this 'scandal.'

Of course, the corrosive effect on the other flight instructors at the training base was building. How could they possibly assign a deserved flight grade to a failing student pilot who could at any time run them off the base and put an end to their careers (not to mention their marriages) by a frivolous 'sexual harassment' charge? And evidence now existed that the command structure would abide and possibly even encourage this action by The Student Pilot. Not only was trust breaking down but the **cold edge of terror** was beginning to invade their professional lives. The instructor pilots could not trust their superior officers to back them up when it counted. To what extent would these superior officers go in demanding that substandard student pilots be passed on to get their coveted Navy 'wings of gold?' As we shall see, some of them would go very far indeed.

Events leading to the Second Progress Review Board

During the period from her second 'down' on 30 April 1995 and her second Progress Review Board on 15 September 1995 (a period of four and one-half months) The Student Pilot continued to have both flying and personal problems. She had grounded herself for emotional reasons for a period of 48 days while undergoing periodic evaluation by three Wing flight surgeons. This was obviously the period during which she and The Lawyers were working out their 'informal' agreement which ended up ruining the career of a young Marine Captain flight instructor.

In addition, after returning to flight status after the first PRB, The Student Pilot received another 'down,' a failed flight awarded on 11 September 1995 during a Fam-19 flight for lining up on the wrong runway during an approach to landing. The Wing Commander, following the advice of his staff, **directed** her instructor pilot to change the 'down' to a 'below average.' The reasoning was that the IP had let the situation (flying to the wrong runway) go too far; therefore, it was as much the IP's fault as The Student Pilot's fault. Consequently, the 'down' was pulled from her official flight training record.

The Student Pilot felt that the IPs in her training squadron were 'out to get her' and asked The Wing Commander for a transfer to the other training squadron in the Wing. Consequently, The Student Pilot resumed flying, this time with the other training squadron in the Wing. The Wing Commander had granted her request to make this change due to her

---

[12] This Marine aviator's career was over. He received orders to a 'transport' squadron, flying the lumbering C-130 cargo and troop-carrier aircraft. He most likely will be able to complete the 20-years active duty requirement for retirement purposes but will surely never be promoted above the rank of Major. His career was quietly derailed. Presumably, this was a better ending than being disciplined on a charge of 'fraternization' and possibly losing even a minimal 'retirement.' And the instigator of the affair, the 'villain' in this fraternization incident, would go scott free. Such is the state of 'fairness' in today's 'feminized' Navy.

'perception' that she was being discriminated against by the flight instructors in her initial training squadron. Indeed, the Navy was walking the extra mile in accommodating every whim and, now, even the 'perception' of discrimination against a naval aviation candidate of a 'protected' or quotaed group -- females.

One week after reporting to the other training squadron, The Student Pilot received another 'down' for <u>again</u> 'flying to the wrong runway.' This time the instructor pilot was the Chief Flight Instructor and no one was going to dispute his call.

This 'down,' her third overall, triggered another formal Progress Review Board to determine the cause of The Student Pilot's continued substandard performance.

The PRB was held on 15 September 1995. It consisted of three naval officers, two naval aviators and a non-voting naval flight surgeon. The PRB reported that The Student Pilot had two 'downs' in the flight familiarization (FAM) stage and her third overall in Phase I of the flight training syllabus. The Student Pilot's grades were below average or marginal in FAM, airways navigation, and radio instruments.

The Student Pilot had below average grades in the FAM stage. Her grade of 3.000 was below the training squadron average of 3.008. She had not completed the more advanced and demanding phases of jet flight training, but her overall Phase I flight grade average of 3.007 was <u>below the overall average</u> of 3.015 for students who had completed this phase. The <u>marginal cutoff grade</u>, that is the <u>minimum grade</u> for successful completion of this phase is 3.009. Thus, The Student Pilot had performed **below the minimum** passing cutoff flying grade. Nevertheless, the <u>PRB decided that</u>:
- The Student Pilot's unsatisfactory performance in FAM-19 was due to 'channeling too much attention' on scanning for the TACAN traffic called by approach control resulting in loss of situational awareness
- The Student Pilot can successfully complete flight training <u>if</u> she is able to develop skills to identify, recover from and cope with mistakes in the air and on the ground
- The flight surgeon advised the board that The Student Pilot had reported to them a 'performance anxiety' which 'had been monitored and treated at the Wing's medical facility.' Reference was made to a '<u>48-day layoff</u>' by The Student Pilot for (unexplained) '<u>personal reasons.</u>'

The board voted 3-0 to <u>retain</u> The Student Pilot and recommended re-flights without ET (extra training). The Student Pilot was being given every benefit of the doubt concerning her difficulties in advanced flight training.

The Student Pilot would later claim, in defense of her flying performance record, that she had passed the 'most demanding part' of naval aviation training -- carrier qualification (CQ) in a jet aircraft. Her attitude was, 'I qualified at the boat so what are you talking about that I am not good enough to be a Navy combat pilot?' Indeed, she completed the carrier qualification part of the jet syllabus in the T-45 jet trainer. She was eligible for this training phase since she had completed the weapons phase.

But The Student Pilot's carrier qualification grades were the lowest in the recent history of the jet training wing. Her CQ grades averaged out to about 2.36, well below the minimum cutoff of 2.9. Her first day at the boat was 'horrible.' Her flying was so poor that the landing signal officer

(LSO) terminated her trials and sat down with her for a sympathetic chat. The next day, he observed an 'improving trend.' This 'improving trend,' a completely subjective judgement, could override her extremely low CQ flying mathematical score. Such subjective judgements had been made many times before for other naval aviation candidates. But never for a candidate with such a low mathematical score. On this basis, however, the LSO passed her through the CQ phase. Later, he would explain to other flight instructors that 'I might just as well pass her. If I don't, someone else will.'

Otherwise, the LSO knew that political pressure from above would be exerted to get the substandard aviator, a member of a politically preferred group, a quotaed group -- females -- through the flight syllabus. Why should he expose himself to friction and confrontation with senior officers by disqualifying The Student Pilot, clearly a substandard aviation candidate? Take the 'easy way' out. In this subtle but practical way, even the most stringent standards -- those for carrier qualification -- have been reduced for females in today's 'feminized' Navy.

During October 1995, after the PRB of 15 September 1995, The Student Pilot reported to the Wing Flight Surgeons. She again claimed to be having 'personal problems' not associated with flying. These Flight Surgeons decided that she needed a psychiatric evaluation at the Navy's premiere Naval Aviation Medical Institute (NAMI) in Pensacola, FL. She had too much personal emotional baggage on her mind to fly. Immediately thereafter, the **flight surgeons grounded her**.

Normally, this situation requires a 90-day 'no fly' period during which a formal psychiatric examination is conducted to determine whether or not the student is a danger to him/herself and/or others. This examination is usually conducted by psychology specialists at NAMI. The Wing Commander, immediately overrode the recommendation of The Flight Surgeons. In addition, he took the following actions:
• Rejected The Flight Surgeons' joint recommendation to have The Student Pilot submit to a psychiatric evaluation at NAMI
• Designated The Student Pilot SERVICE GROUP 1, physically and aeronautically adapted for flight immediately.

In December 1995, the Naval Aviation Safety Center called one of the Wing Flight Surgeons who had recommended grounding The Student Pilot. They asked if she had been **flying while in a grounded status**. A similar conversation must have taken place between the Naval Aviation Safety Center and The Wing Commander. Immediately thereafter, pressure was applied on The Flight Surgeons to alter their 'grounding' recommendation.

The Wing Chief Staff Officer (CSO), the direct subordinate of The Wing Commander, pressured the three Flight Surgeons to give The Student Pilot an 'up-chit' to continue flight training. This would relieve pressure on the Wing Commander who had countermanded their original recommendation. In a rather abusive confrontation with The Flight Surgeons, the CSO threatened them with 'orders to Bosnia' if they refused his request. It was obvious to The Flight Surgeons that the CSO had received his marching orders from the Wing Commander. But The Flight Surgeons would not back down. They remained steadfast in their recommendation that The Student Pilot should be grounded for psychological reasons.

Under severe pressure from The Wing Commander, The Flight Surgeons undertook further examination of The Student Pilot in order to determine whether or not they had been too harsh in their original recommendation. During these sessions, The Student Pilot gave her famous 'big wide-eyed boo-hoo' story in an attempt to influence the three Flight Surgeons to give her an up-chit and return to flying status. She had nearly convinced the two male flight surgeons who were leaning toward 'letting her off the hook.' The female flight surgeon told the two male flight surgeons that they were being conned. It was clear to her that 'you guys are being suckered' by The Student Pilot. The Flight Surgeons then stood firm in their original judgement, a recommendation to ground The Student Pilot. The Flight Surgeons again recommended a formal psychological examination at NAMI.

In the meantime, The Wing Commander wrote to the Chief of Naval Air Training (CNATRA) outlining how they might '<u>handle</u>' The Student Pilot's situation without a formal psychological medical examination at NAMI. The Wing Commander argued against a formal NAMI examination of The Student Pilot. CNATRA wrote back with a sharp rejoinder, essentially saying 'Don't tell me how to <u>handle</u> The Student Pilot, <u>just give me your recommendation whether or not to attrit her.</u>'

During this same general time frame, a U.S. Naval Academy friend of The Student Pilot, who had completed advanced flight training and who was undergoing Fleet Replacement Squadron (FRS) training in the F/A-18 Hornet at Lemoore, CA, visited her. He drove from Lemoore to El Centro, CA where The Student Pilot was on detachment for ordnance training at the practice bombing range there. He had heard that she was having difficulty in her flight training and thought he might be able to provide some aid and comfort.

After visiting with The Student Pilot, it became known that this Navy LT 'was worried that The Student Pilot was so emotionally troubled that she **may commit suicide.**' Here the story becomes a bit 'fuzzy,' but it is clear that it became known to the Commanding Officer and the Executive Officer (XO) of the LT's FRS at Lemoore. It appears that an inkling of the story also became known to a flight surgeon[13] at The Student Pilot's training base. A flight surgeon there apparently followed up on 'rumors' of this episode by calling the Executive Officer of the FRS. This call precipitated a phone call from the XO of the FRS to a senior officer at The Student Pilot's training base, inquiring of the matter. A senior officer at the training base called The Flight Surgeons to inquire of the information that he had learned from NAS Lemoore. It was obvious to all that the apparent 'suicide' reference concerning The Student Pilot would be pertinent information for consideration by NAMI.

By this time, the Navy LT at Lemoore had obtained legal counsel and refused to verify the story he had told his superior officers of The Student Pilot's reference to 'suicide.' In fact, he apparently denied (before his Commanding Officer back at Lemoore -- in the presence of a lawyer) that he had said anything about 'suicide' to anyone. The details of this part of the episode are not known at the naval air training base in this story. The details are known, however, by senior Navy officers who were in the FRS at NAS Lemoore at the time.

Since any hint of talk of **'suicide'** in naval aviation is of extreme importance and urgency in determining whether or not there is a <u>safety-of-</u>

---

[13] This story is well known to the Commanding Officer and the Executive Officer of the
F/A-18 Fleet Replacement Squadron at Lemoore, CA at the time. They interacted with senior officers at The Student Pilot's training base. The CO and XO of the FRS at Lemoore know the full details of this episode. As time evolved, others also became aware of this episode.

flight problem, any under-the-table handling of this matter is of grave concern. Nevertheless, this incident has been completely hushed up at both the naval air training base in this story and at NAS Lemoore. NAMI would never learn of this episode.

It is at this time that The Wing Commander, contrary to his order in October 1995, recommended to CNATRA that The Student Pilot be sent to Pensacola, FL for a NAMI 'psychiatric evaluation.' The results of this 'evaluation' are reported below. As we shall see, The Wing Commander had covered his backside with his boss, the Admiral, while manipulating the process so that The Student Pilot could maintain her flight status and pursue her wings of gold. The Wing Commander was developing an <u>obsession</u> with 'winging' this obviously 'flawed' fledgling female aviator. His <u>obsession</u> was beginning to match her own.

In preparation for The Student Pilot's psychiatric examination, NAMI asked for her training records, including all flight performance evaluations as well as local reports of 'personal problems.' As a result, The Flight Instructors in the Wing wrote up a detailed summary of The Student Pilot's flying performance at the training base. The Wing Commander cancelled this action. Consequently, no flight instructor input was available to the 'psychiatric evaluators.'

Since no flight instructor input (which described her substandard flight performance and 'downs' at the naval aviation training base) was sent to NAMI, the medical examiners there gave The Student Pilot a 'thumbs up' to continue flying. This was based primarily on The Student Pilot's obvious enthusiasm for (obsession with) continuing her flight training. NAMI had no other choice.

During the NAMI deliberations on their psychiatric examination of The Student Pilot, The Wing Commander took two cross-country flights to Pensacola, FL to consult with the NAMI medical evaluators. His influence was heavily felt in their decision. He is known for his 'back-door' maneuvering in such matters. According to those familiar with his career, he is a master at manipulating the system in favor of female and minority student pilots. He is, in fact, part of a very tight-knit network of Navy equal-opportunity (EO) officers which reaches the highest level -- into the office of the Chief of Naval Operations.

The Third Progress Review Board for The Student Pilot
It is perfectly within Navy regulations for a Wing Commander to override the recommendation of his flight surgeons in determining the flight status of his student pilots. However, any Wing Commander who decides to override this recommendation runs the risk of subsequent events raising questions concerning his judgement. In this case, while flying in a 'grounded flight status,' The Student Pilot received a number of further 'downs.' After five official and recorded 'downs' in her flight jacket and up to four more 'unofficial' or 'excused' 'downs' (for a total of nine 'downs') The Wing Commander was required[14] to give The Student Pilot another Progress Review Board.

On 21 May 1996, the third Progress Review Board was convened for The Student Pilot. This board consisted of five members; a new Wing Chief Staff Officer (CSO), a LCDR female Operations Officer from a training squadron at

---

[14] It is mandatory that a Progress Review Board be convened when a naval aviation candidate is awarded five 'downs.'

another naval air training base, a reservist CDR who flies for American Airlines in civilian life, and two flight instructors who were directly familiar with the flight performance of The Student Pilot at the naval air training base of this story.

Before the board started its deliberations, the CSO read a communication from some higher authority. This communication contained the <u>order</u>, "*If you don't decide to keep her, you must recommend her for a pipeline change to the maritime (propeller-driven aircraft) community. You must give her a chance to earn her wings there.*" Such high-level command-authority interference in an evaluation board's deliberations is unethical at best and illegal at worst. A Progress Review Board is supposed to be a completely independent body, free from 'command influence' or any other 'political influence.' The CSO, a direct subordinate of the Wing Commander, who chaired the PRB was obviously carrying out the orders of either his immediate superior or orders from a higher authority.

The board voted 5-0 to attrit The Student Pilot out of the advanced jet aviation pipeline. A major disagreement followed in the decision as to whether or not The Student Pilot should be given a transition to the turbojet E2/C2 pipeline, where students are trained to fly a less demanding twin engine turboprop early warning/cargo delivery aircraft. But these aircraft also operate off aircraft carriers, not the safest flying environment for a marginal pilot.

The female operations officer stated that 'I think The Student Pilot has what it takes to be in the maritime community.' Her vote was recorded for transition to the E2/C2. The CSO voted for transition to the E2/C2. He was obviously carrying out the wishes of the Wing Commander who knew that The Student Pilot wanted E2/C2 training in the event that she were to be attrited from the jet aviation program. It was known that The Student Pilot was already studying the E2/C2 training syllabus just in case she might be attrited from jet training. Nevertheless, she was still holding out for continuation of advanced jet training. The CSO's vote was recorded for a pipeline transition to the E2/C2 program.

The reserve CDR, who had recently been promoted to CDR in the Reserves, was also subject to political pressure from above. He was under consideration to replace the outgoing CO of the reserve unit at the training base. The Flight Instructors at the base believed that he was placed on the board as a kind of 'you scratch my back and I'll scratch yours' situation. He voted for a transition to the E2/C2 pipeline. His vote was very suspect by The Flight Instructors at the base. Within a few months of the PRB, he was the new CO of the reserve squadron.

The two flight instructors, the only members of the board with direct familiarity with the flight record of The Student Pilot, voted against a maritime pipeline change to the E2/C2 program. Their arguments made sense. A pipeline change to the E2-C2 community would imperil not only the substandard pilot but up to six or more crew members or passengers in an airplane which is arguably one of the most difficult to land aboard ship. Its large wingspan renders the E2/C2 aircraft quite vulnerable to lineup errors during a carrier approach because of the small margin of wingtip clearance between the aircraft and ship-board structures. Consequently, the flight instructors on the review board strongly recommended against any 'tailhook' future for The Student Pilot, given their knowledge of her weakness in FAM and Phase I performance. In their view, The Student Pilot would never make it in the 'tailhook' Navy. She would be a danger to herself and others.

These flight instructors pointed out that CNATRA Instruction 1500.4E, which outlines who is eligible to transition to the maritime pipeline, specifically calls for only two cases which warrant consideration for a maritime pipeline transition. Neither of these cases applied to The Student Pilot. They are:
- Skill deficiency in field carrier landing practice (FCLP) or carrier landing phase, but <u>otherwise satisfactory flight performance</u>. The Student Pilot's case was exactly obverse to this provision. She had barely squeezed through CQ with the lowest grades in recent history but had not exhibited an 'otherwise satisfactory flight performance.' If she had exhibited such a flying record, she would not be before her third Performance Review Board.
- Aeromedical reasons (e.g. throwing up under high g-loads). The Student Pilot had no such problem.

Furthermore, it is well understood in advanced naval carrier aviation that a student pilot cannot merely request a transition due to poor performance in jet aviation training. The maritime community does not want jet aviation training's rejects.

Obviously, none of these cases applied to The Student Pilot. So the board voted a result that did not conform to the CNATRA Instruction. How could this be justified? The flight instructors on the PRB could not rationalize an honest answer to this question. Neither could any other flight instructor at the base who knew the details of the situation. An obvious major degradation in naval aviation qualification standards was being implemented right before their very eyes.

The view of The Flight Instructors was that, if The Student Pilot doesn't have what it takes, it's better they find it out now, during jet aviation training, than out in the fleet. In the fleet, substandard carrier naval aviators would most likely make fatal mistakes resulting in death or injury to themselves and others. Or, if lucky, they would be subject to evaluation boards (FNAEBs) that would make the final decision to ground them before they killed themselves. But the latter path takes up valuable time and energy in operational air wings, diminishing their effectiveness and operational readiness.

These Flight Instructors did not view The Student Pilot, herself, as the problem. Instead, they believed the problem to be the Navy's current training system which practices reverse discrimination. They were nearly unanimous that 'affirmative action' has lowered the training and qualification standards, that is, has set double standards which have damaged the Navy.

The Aftermath of the Third Progress Review Board

It took over two months before the results of the PRB were released to either The Student Pilot or the rest of the Training Wing. This is extraordinary. Usually, only a few days pass before the official results of a Progress Review Board are announced. After the 3-2 decision for a pipeline transition to the maritime program, concurrence had to be obtained from the Commodore of the maritime pipeline TRAWING. But the Maritime TRAWING Commander refused to take The Student Pilot. In fact, the senior flight surgeon for the Maritime TRAWING said, 'If she comes here, I will not give her an up-chit to fly.' Obviously, he had talked to some flight surgeon in The Student Pilot's Training Wing. It became clear that the maritime pipeline commander would not take jet aviation's 'rejects,' especially one so far below the Navy's aviation standards.

So, with that avenue blocked, The Wing Commander decided to try to get The Student Pilot into the Navy's E6-A (the civilian passenger Boeing 707 converted to serve as the submarine force communication TACAMO aircraft) program. They informally inquired of the Air Force, which trains student pilots in the E-6 for the Navy, to accept her into that training program. But they found that she had to earn her 'wings' in a naval aviation training program before the Air Force would accept her. And she could not be 'winged' in the Navy until she passed some **minimum** standard in the Navy's advanced flight training program. Such a dilemma for an obsessive student pilot and a Navy command structure which finds it extremely difficult to 'wash out' a substandard female or minority aviation candidate, a member of a quotaed group.

While awaiting the announcement of the PRB's conclusions, The Student Pilot was flying in the 'back seat' with instructor pilots who were conducting other training. She had obtained The Wing Commander's permission and orders to do so. This was a continuation of past leniency given her by The Wing Commander in obtaining 'extra flight time' in the back seat. Up to her last PRB, The Student Pilot had accumulated 90 hours extra flight time in the 'back seat.' She had also accumulated 35 such 'special' flights prior to her starting the ACM (air-combat maneuvers) stage.

But this new situation was different. She was now in a 'grounded' status while the results of the third PRB were being deliberated up the chain-of-command. CNATRA Instruction 1500.4 states that '...*a Student Naval Aviator shall stop flying when in a down status. This includes 'back seat' flights. Training will not continue until the final disposition of the PRB.*" The Flight Instructors at the advanced aviation training base know of no student who was ever allowed to continue flying while awaiting the final outcome of a PRB.

Now, while flying in the 'back seat,' The Student Pilot was not only flying against precedent and written Navy Instructions, she was taking valuable flight time from 'candidate' instructor pilots under training to be flight instructors. Many IPs were refusing to let The Student Pilot fly in their 'back seat' flights while she was in a 'grounded' PRB status at the expense of IP training. The Wing Commander, upon learning this, issued the following threat. "*Any IP who will not let [The Student Pilot] fly in his back seat, and his Commanding Officer, will immediately submit their resignation letters to him immediately...*" Indeed, **intimidation and fear** were now being used daily as tools to enforce quotas in today's 'affirmative action' Navy.

Many naval aviators of long experience were flabbergasted at the lengths to which the Navy went to accommodate a substandard female aviation candidate. What possible leverage could she have to move the entire Navy like this? How could the **minimum** qualification standards be so blatantly lowered to accommodate a member of a politically preferred group? Is the radical feminist political pressure on the Navy so feared by its leaders that this has come to pass? The answer, in the wake of Tailhook '91, their tactical rallying point, has been YES!

As her difficulties with the flight training program continued, the Navy prepared a list of those instructors who could no longer fly with The Student Pilot. This is standard practice in naval aviation training. Such a list customarily includes all the flight instructors who have previously given the student a down, or failing grade -- the reasoning is that perhaps they will no longer be objective.

In this case, also included on the list were all those flight instructors who had sat on Progress Review Boards to determine if The Student Pilot should continue flight training. And one day, as the list sat on the Scheduling Officer's desk, several flight instructors who were angered by the command's leniency with The Student Pilot, apparently added their names to the list as well.

In the meantime, The Student Pilot became concerned that the Navy might indeed 'wash her out' of the program. Consequently, she enlisted the aid of a team of lawyers, some of whom may have been attached to or sympathetic with the **WANDAS** group[15,16] which seeks out and takes legal and political advantage of such cases. Political pressure could be placed on the Navy command structure to allow The Student Pilot to continue her quest for her coveted 'wings of gold.' As of late Summer of 1996, the Navy maintained a curious silence on her 21 May 1996 Progress Review Board. It had been far behind the normal schedule in making its deliberations known. Fears flowed through the Navy command structure that The Student Pilot, supported by WANDAS, might file a 'discrimination' law suit if the decision was not to her liking. The mood at the naval aviation training base became tense. What was the Navy command structure up to? How high in the chain of command would this decision go?

Higher Authority's Consideration of the PRB Conclusions

In early July 1996, after an extensive review of the Progress Review Board's conclusions and The Wing Commander's recommendations, CNATRA sent a memo to The Wing Commander which essentially said, *'The Student Pilot is done.'* CNATRA had reviewed her flight jacket and determined that The Student Pilot's problem was *'poor headwork, which makes it a safety of flight issue.'* Subsequently, The Student Pilot was *'put on hold.'* In the meantime, it had become common knowledge at the Wing that The Wing Commander had prepared for CNATRA's review, along with the PRB conclusions, a 'sanitized version' of The Student Pilot's flight jacket, absent any description or record of the four 'excused downs.' Evidently, someone sent, through the back door to CNATRA, the flight records of these 'excused downs' awarded The Student Pilot. Consequently, CNATRA determined that 'pulling the downs' from her official record was not the proper thing to have done.

Upon learning the results of CNATRA's preliminary decision, The Student Pilot was granted (at her request) an Admiral's Mast with CNATRA. It is rumored that she told the Admiral that she believed that certain flight instructors were 'after her.' And presumably, that was the sole reason for her poor flying performance. On this basis, CNATRA granted the opportunity for The Student Pilot to make her case.

---

15   Associated Press, "Group organizes to fight military sex harassment," The Providence Journal, 13 June 1994. This surreptitious radical feminist group is based in Denver, CO and is an offshoot of Rep. Patricia Schroeder's feminist network. It is headed by a militant feminist lawyer, Susan Barnes. This informal network is activated by radical feminists through a quasi-secret organization called **WANDAS** (Women Active in our Nation's Defense, their Advocates and Supporters). This network, whose members are primarily *"lawyers, accountants, psychiatrists, politicians, and lobbyists"* also include **anonymous active-duty female naval officers!** This 'secret' organization exerts subversive pressure on Senate approval of officer promotions and intimidates Navy officers who are not sufficiently supportive of the feminization of the U.S. Navy.

16   Brooke, James, "New Attention to Women in Military," The New York Times, 3 March 1997.

The Student Pilot's Reclama and Submission of 'Human Factors' Reconsideration

The Student Pilot requested an 'Admiral's Mast' with CNATRA, which was granted and conducted on 15 July 1996. At that meeting, she gave the Admiral a list of names of flight instructors who she believed were 'after her,' that is, were determined to wash her out of the program. Her two-page list contained names of instructor pilots and gave a myriad of past 'slights,' 'aggravations,' and 'grievances' she had experienced while at the naval aviation training base.

The Wing Commander had directly assisted The Student Pilot in formulating this list. In concert with The Student Pilot's 'reclama' of her pending attrition from flight training based on CNATRA's review decision, The Wing Commander sent an official request to CNATRA requesting either, 1) a pipeline change for The Student Pilot to the E2/C2 program (a tailhook billet which was expressly counter to the judgement of the Wing flight instructors on the PRB who were familiar with her flying qualities), or 2) a relaxation of standards within the Air Wing to 'wing' The Student Pilot **short of her actually qualifying** by completion of the entire flight syllabus. Since her most recent failure was in the Air Combat Maneuver (ACM) phase[17], he would 'waive' the 3-plane ACM requirement, 'wing' her, and send her to the E-6A program. As a backup to this move or a move to the E2/C2 pipeline, he would consider 'winging' her and send her to the Navy's anti-submarine training program to fly S-3s, the Navy's jet twin-engine anti-submarine aircraft. Of course, this aircraft operates from the decks of aircraft carriers, flying at night and poor weather conditions at low altitudes. The Wing Commander's obsession with 'winging' this flawed naval aviation candidate was becoming bizarre.

Incredibly, The Wing Commander had gone on record requesting that The Student Pilot be 'given' her Navy 'wings of gold' <u>without actually earning them</u>. That is, the Student Pilot would <u>not</u> be required to complete the flying syllabus that all other student pilots were required to complete before receiving their coveted 'wings of gold.' This request represented not only a double standard for women and minorities in naval aviation but a **complete absence of standards.**

There are no standards in the U.S. Navy when mid-level equal employment opportunity (EEO) 'affirmative action' milicrats trash the established standards to reach their goals (quotas) for special privileged groups. But the climate is such within the U.S. Navy today that these 'affirmative action' milicrats actually enhance their promotion potential and careers by carrying out such insidious agendas. Their careers flourish, morale takes a dive, and the U.S. Navy becomes a hollow fighting force.

On 15 July 1996, CNATRA turned down the Wing Commander's formal request, citing The Student Pilot's 'unsafe flight performance.' He also cited that the Wing Commander of the maritime pipeline (the E2/C2 pipeline) had conducted his own review of The Student Pilot's flight training record and recommended disapproval of a change to either pipeline. This citation led to CNATRA's concurrence with this Commander. CNATRA's official decision did not, however, satisfy either The Student Pilot or The Wing Commander.

The Student Pilot and The Wing Commander immediately set to work to negate CNATRA's decision. It is clear that this action would attempt to go

---

[17] The Student Pilot had failed to notify her fellow combatants, via radio calls, that she had lost sight of them during relatively violent and rapidly changing air combat maneuvers. This failure gravely endangered her and her wingmen. This is a damning 'no, no' during air combat maneuvers.

around as well as through the chain of command, possibly all the way up to the Chief of Naval Operations (through the back-channel of the EEO network which The Wing Commander had at his fingertips).

The Navy Invokes an Inspector General Investigation

The Wing Commander set in motion an informal 'fact-finding' investigation of the circumstances described in The Student Pilot's 28-page 'human factors' accusations against Wing flight instructors. This investigation became known later as CNATRA's 'Inspector General (IG)' investigation. Its name was later changed in order that it not be releasable to the public via a freedom of information act request. This investigation was conducted by CNATRA's Chief of Staff on Thursday 22 August 1996. Without formally swearing-in[18] those interviewed, CNATRA's CSO attempted to ascertain two things; 1) was there a laxity in the professional and 'social' climate at the aviation training base that may have led to 'fraternization' among student pilots and flight instructors, and 2) whether or not there was substance to The Student Pilot's 'human factors' claims of discrimination against her by flight instructors. CNATRA's CSO appeared satisfied that the answer to the second question was NEGATIVE. Only minor 'nit-picks' of little substance were evident. All flight instructors interviewed were cleared of any charge of 'discrimination.' It is not clear how the first question was resolved.

The 22 August 'informal' IG investigation also addressed the so-called 'secret list.' This list purported to contain the names of flight instructors who had placed their names there as a statement of refusal to fly with The Student Pilot. More than one name on this list was there absent the knowledge of the person named. Obviously, this list was not as it was purported to be by The Student Pilot[19]. Somehow, this list was a bogus list of names trumped up and added to a list of names of IPs who had previously given The Student Pilot an unsatisfactory flight evaluation. As previously explained, the latter is a normal practice invoked to protect any naval aviation candidate from bias, personal or other wise, during flight training. A CNATRA instruction advises that, if a flight instructor gives a student one 'down,' in one stage of flight training, he is not allowed to fly with that student again in that stage (but may fly with the student in a different stage) for fear of having prejudiced his judgement by the experience of the first failed flight. In practice, most instructor pilots

---

[18] This action suggests a complete absence of intent to ascertain violations of the Uniform Code of Military Justice during the investigation. The information gained would simply be used to ascertain 'what was going on' at the Wing and how procedures might be improved if problems were determined to exist.

[19] The Wing Commander had included this 'secret list' in the 'package' which The Student Pilot submitted to CNATRA in support of her 'human factors' reclama to his decision to attrit her. The Wing Commander had earlier shown this list to 'outside' sources, claiming that the list was an example of something that had been 'misunderstood' and an illustration of what WAS NOT done wrong in his handling of the episode. The Flight Instructors, however, tell a different story. Theirs is an account of The Wing Commander continually using the list as a means of threatening them with a career-ending IG investigation -- long before it was finally cleared up by the CNATRA 'informal' investigation. If The Wing Commander had cleared it up to his and the Navy's satisfaction before the CNATRA IG investigation, why had he included it in the 'package' that he helped prepare for The Student Pilot's 'human factors' reclama? The Wing Commander simply displayed here his propensity to speak out of both sides of his mouth -- to cover his trail if this story ever emerged outside the Navy.

will not fly with a student in other stages, if practicable, so as not to put pressure on them. This procedure properly protects the interests of naval aviation candidates.

The fact is that the existence of such a 'secret list' was promoted by a flight instructor who was trying to curry favor with both The Wing Commander (a career interest) and The Student Pilot (a sexual interest). This flight instructor, twice divorced, had flown an over-night cross-country flight with The Student Pilot and shared a motel room with her (instead of separate rooms). He was obviously using his 'mistaken knowledge' of a 'secret list' to curry sexual favor[20] with The Student Pilot. This knowledge turned out to be flawed by mistaken identity of the existence and nature of the official 'no-refly' list.

The informal IG investigation straightened this matter out to the satisfaction of the investigating officers from CNATRA. This whole tale, however, reveals how Byzantine and complex the mixing-of-the-sexes has become in the U.S. military. Men will still participate in despicable acts to curry favor with certain females. Females will encourage this favor and take advantage of it to further their own ends. Such is human nature. Such activities have been observed (both ways) for over 6,000 years of the recorded history of mankind. Today, somehow we imagine that all of human experience can be engineered to a different mold -- only to be disappointed when nature takes its revenge.

It very quickly became evident that the direction taken by the 'informal' IG investigation displeased The Wing Commander. His efforts on behalf of the failed female student aviator were beginning to look ridiculous to his superiors, even those who were carrying out the Navy's politically correct agenda for women-in-combat. Driven by his obsession, he had to find a way to stifle criticism of his actions and his decisions. Well known for his proclivity to 'fly off the handle' and 'go bananas' when faced with adverse situations, The Wing Commander reacted to a threat to his career in the acclaimed fashion. He raised the level of conflict.

On Friday, 23 August 1996, the day after the 'informal' IG investigation was conducted, The Wing Commander set in motion an investigation of a far more serious nature. At least one senior officer and at least one flight instructor were summoned before a <u>formal</u> IG investigation, conducted by the same CNATRA Chief Staff Officer. The Chief of Naval Education and Training (CNET), CNATRA's immediate superior, had been informed that a reporter was doing a story on this whole affair and

---

[20] This practice of female naval aviation candidates taking over-night cross-country training flights with male flight instructors appears to be a common practice at this naval aviation training base. In addition, The Student Pilot was living in a house off-base with three males and another female. The males were all instructor pilots. The females were all students. All of this behavior is a flagrant and gross violation of the military's well-known and strict **fraternization** rules between junior and more senior officers. These rules are very strict when the officers are in the same chain of command. They are directly appropriate when the senior officers, in this case the flight instructors, are in a position of authority and control over the career of the junior officers. When confronted with this fact by The Wing Commander, The Student Pilot professed complete innocence and saw nothing wrong with this 'arrangement.' Obviously, this new generation of 'Friends,' the popular NBC-TV program where everyone lives together, has sex outside marriage, and thinks this behavior normal, is imprinting its pop-culture on the Navy.

apparently had possession of some documents supporting the story. As we shall see, The Wing Commander (in conjunction with The Student Pilot) was the source of this accusation. At least one of the accused flight instructors was formally and legally 'sworn-in' for testimony that could be used in a disciplinary hearing under the Uniform Code of Military Justice. The source of the 'leak' would be found and punished. At least one of the accused refused to waive his rights and undertook to engage an attorney as a legal defense. The accused were neither notified of the identity of their accuser(s) nor the charges against them. They were simply notified that they had been 'identified.' It is clear that the identifiers were both the Wing Commander and The Student Pilot, acting in conjunction on pure wild conjecture.

How had this turn of events come to pass? It involved The Reporter. The Reporter had, a week earlier (15 August 1996), interviewed face-to-face The Wing Commander, concerning the whole episode involving the substandard flying performance of The Student Pilot. The interview was 'off the record.' It is clear, however, that much of the story concerning The Student Pilot must have been corroborated during this interview. In fact, The Wing Commander is publicly known to give minorities and women extra chances. He has admitted that he goes overboard for minorities and women to get them through flight training.

It is widely rumored that, during this interview, The Wing Commander showed The Reporter a 'package' (The Student Pilot's 'human factors' reclama) that he had prepared for The Student Pilot to send to CNATRA rebutting his decision to wash her out of flight training. Many naval officers have viewed the contents of this 'package.' Its contents are well-known to staff officers and other Navy officers at the base. This 'package' contained a so-called 'secret list' of flight instructors, some of whom had allegedly 'discriminated' against her during her tenure at the base. This list became a part of the subject of the informal IG investigation of the flight instructors wherein the charges were judged to be frivolous and without merit by the CNMATRA CSO on 22 August. Many who have seen this 'secret list' noted that some of the names on it were 'in the same handwriting' and could not have been placed there by the individual whose name appeared there.

It is now clear how the abrupt change occurred between 22 August and 23 August, changing the venue from an informal 'fact-finding' to a formal and legal IG investigation of The Student Pilot's and The Wing Commander's fraudulent accusation. On 22 August 1996, the very day of the informal investigation, The Reporter had called The Wing Commander and challenged him to go 'on the record' with his previous 'off the record' comments. The Reporter apparently had or had seen 'documents' related to The Student Pilot's story which confirmed what The Wing Commander had told The Reporter 'off the record.' The Wing Commander had obviously conveyed this information to his superiors, including CNET (Chief of Navy Education and Training), who called for CNATRA to convene a **formal** IG investigation of the matter. The Wing Commander was obviously determined that the public not learn the details of this story and his sorry role in it.

The Wing Commander was not the only one at the command who was violently opposed to media coverage of The Student Pilot's situation. In fact, The Student Pilot threatened to sue The Reporter and The Newspaper if a story about her was published.

By the end of the day, Friday 23 August 1996, after the formal IG investigation had been initiated that morning, The Wing Commander had second thoughts (probably after conversations with CNATRA) and agreed that the formal IG investigation be cancelled. It was clear by then, even to him, that The Student Pilot's claims were frivolous and could not be substantiated by fact. But by then, it became clear that The Wing Commander had gone much too far in his pursuit of 'affirmative action' on behalf of unqualified aviation candidates. It became clear to all that a **campaign of terror** was being waged on an innocent victim of The Wing Commander's excess.

The Commanding Officer of one of the Wing training squadrons had acquired a complete set of information with names, places, dates, and times of the whole set of problems relating to The Student Pilot and others during his tenure at the naval air training base. He let it be known that this information would be made public if The Wing Commander continued his vendetta in favor of The Student Pilot.

At this time it became known that The Student Pilot had retained an attorney, possibly assisted by the radical feminist group, WANDAS. It is widely known at the naval aviation training base, including attorneys hired by the targets of the formal IG investigation, that if the IG investigation story should ever come out, including The Student Pilot's 'fraternization' history, then The Lawyers would drop her as indefensible. The Student Pilot had too much baggage to be taken before the American people as a model for the feminist agenda. She would not hold up even under the low standards of 'Nightline' or other biased national media outlets. The commanding officer of the training squadron had presumably told The Wing Commander that he had retained an attorney and, when the IG investigation was over and the issue died down, he might file charges against The Student Pilot for making false official statements. The Wing Commander's vendetta against his own instructor pilots was coming unglued.

The Reporter Tried to 'Do the Right Thing'

Meanwhile The Reporter continued to research the story. However, the threat of a lawsuit made the editors of The Newspaper reluctant to publish it. The Newspaper would delay publishing the story until after the Navy's formal report on the 'informal' IG investigation was completed. The reporter filed a Freedom of Information Act (FOIA) request with CNATRA for the 'informal' IG investigation report. This request was made during the first week in September 1996.

As the IG investigation report worked its way up the chain of command, through CNET and presumably all the way up to the Chief of Naval Operations (CNO), The Reporter continued to press The Editor for publication of this important story. During this time, The Wing Commander became increasingly hostile to The Reporter. He did not relish the idea of a story coming out which would be critical of his role in lowering the **minimum** qualification standards for such an obviously substandard female aviation candidate.

The Student Pilot, revealing a deep obsession to earn her wings at any cost, continued to hold out hopes for a pipeline transfer to the E2/C2 program. The Navy chain of command was staring at the same kind of situation that had cost ADM Stanley Arthur his promotion to command of the U.S. Pacific Forces when ADM Jeremy Boorda (the Chief of Naval Operations (CNO) at the time) essentially 'fired' ADM Arthur and 'hired' LT Rebecca Hanson, a failed helicopter pilot trainee[21].

---

[21] Boyer, Peter J., "What Killed Admiral Boorda: Admiral Boorda's War," The New Yorker, pp. 68, 16 September 1996.

It would appear that the final decision on The Student Pilot would be made at the top of the Navy chain of command, given the extremely sensitive political climate in Washington, DC wherein radical feminists and their allies in the Clinton administration and Congress were violating the traditional U.S. Navy officer promotion[22,23] process all the way down through Lieutenant (O-3)[24].

During the second week in October 1996, The Reporter learned from CNATRA's legal staff that the Navy would not release any part of the IG investigation report to the public. The Navy cited three exceptions to the Freedom of Information Act (FOIA) law that allowed this unusual exclusionary position;
    1) <u>Privacy considerations</u> for The Student Pilot and others
    2) <u>Law enforcement provision</u> (including **criminal** matters), although no charges had been filed. Presumably this exception was invoked on the basis of a possible 'sexual harassment' charge that had been hanging in the wind for many months and still not <u>legally</u> resolved
    3) <u>Revelations of internal decisions</u> of Navy authorities.
Consequently, The Newspaper was faced with the decision of whether or not to print the story without the Navy's IG investigation report.

During the third week of September 1996, The Reporter requested and received a meeting with CNATRA. CNATRA requested that their conversation be 'off the record.' This is understood to mean 'use the information but without attribution to the source.' CNATRA would not release the IG investigation report to The Reporter. Consequently, The Reporter would not be able to authoritatively write a story on The Student Pilot. The Navy would successfully cover up the whole sordid affair -- just as it had covered up the fact of double standards in qualifying the first crop of female combat pilots (the LT Kara Hultgreen affair). The public would never know of this perfidy.

It was well known among the staff officers at CNATRA and the TRAWING that, at this time, CNATRA's decision had not changed but he was still handling the matter gingerly since The Student Pilot had not yet been notified. Presumably, the Navy was worried that she might take legal action against it. But at this time a full <u>four months</u> had passed since the conclusion of the Progress Review Board and <u>two months</u> after CNATRA's initial decision to attrit The Student Pilot. Nevertheless, his decision had not changed from that made during mid-July 1996 -- attrit The Student Pilot without a pipeline change to E2/C2s or maritime propeller-driven

---

22   See Gerald L. Atkinson, 'The New Totalitarians: Bosnia as a Mirror of America's Future,' Atkinson Associates Press, P.O. Box 1417, Clinton, MD 20735, 1996, for a detailed review of the violation of the Navy's traditional promotion process by the radical feminists and their allies in the Clinton administration and Congress, especially on the Senate Armed Services Committee which approves officer promotions. Totalitarian procedures, invoked without due process by the Department of Defense, opened the process to unsubstantiated and false accusations against naval aviators. This process started with a corrupt investigation of the Tailhook '91 'scandal' and ended with the infiltration of Senate Staff, including that of the Senate Armed Services Committee, the Pentagon, the White House, and the U.S. Navy with radical feminists carrying out a destructive political agenda.
23   Cohen, Richard, "Keelhauling Commander Stumpf: Not all the victims of Tailhook were women," The Washington Post, 12 January 1996.
24   Caldwell, Robert J., "Another Tailhook atrocity: The case of the man who wasn't there," Insight Section, The San Diego Union-Tribune, 18 February 1996.

aircraft. But obviously this decision had to be vetted all the way up the chain of command. The ADM Boorda/ADM Arthur/LT Hansen case had rendered the Navy, at the highest level, very sensitive to the political danger inherent in a radical feminist charge of 'discrimination' against a female in the new Navy.

These same staff officers have observed CNATRA acknowledge that the major issue with The Student Pilot centered around **fraternization**. After The Student Pilot had leveled the 'sexual harassment' charge against a flight instructor at the naval aviation training base, the other flight instructors became skittish about honestly grading her flight performance when she flew poorly. In addition, CNATRA has said that he was looking into the social atmosphere at the naval air training base with respect to 'fraternization.' Maybe the social climate between students, especially female students, and male flight instructors was too lax. Presumably, The Wing Commander had something to do with this lax social environment[25].

In addition, CNATRA has observed to others that The Student Pilot had received twice as much flying time as other students and she had still not progressed satisfactorily. She had been undergoing jet training for over 20 months (she was only in Phase I) in the training syllabus whereas the norm to completion, including the more difficult Air Combat Maneuvers phase, is only ten months.

CNATRA has observed to these same staff officers that The Student Pilot's case was remarkably like Rebecca Hansen's (the failed helicopter pilot who finally got ADM Stanley Arthur fired), but Hansen was a failed pilot and a bad officer (went outside the Navy chain of command). The Student Pilot was a failed pilot but a 'good officer,' who was staying inside the Navy chain of command.

CNATRA has further acknowledged that the story of The Student Pilot's travails had travelled outside the training command. He would naturally feel slightly 'betrayed' by this fact. But, he has observed to others that maybe The Flight Instructors felt that they had tried to talk to him (through their superiors) and maybe they didn't feel it got passed on to him. It is known that CNATRA refused to punish any flight instructor who may have talked to 'outsiders.' He has observed to others that the Navy was learning and maybe things were working out the right way[26].

---

[25] In fairness to The Wing Commander, it should be pointed out that the 'lax social environment' at the base, if indeed one existed, was started long before The Wing Commander's arrival on the scene. The previous wing commander had been a primary actor in framing the social scene at the base. Things may have slowly 'gotten out of hand' as a result of attempting to make female officers 'feel at home' and 'welcome' in a Navy which was trying its darndest to accommodate them into the traditionally male-dominated institution.

[26] Many senior naval officers, both active-duty and retired, may believe that this whole story is, in fact, proof that the Navy acted properly. After all, a sub-standard naval aviation candidate was finally attrited. But it is not clear that this would have been the result had CNATRA not made a decision to retire. Had he wished to stay on active duty and compete for the next level in his career, he would have been subject to the same political pressure, both inside and outside the Navy, that is destroying the institution. He would have been driven by the same **campaign of terror** which is immobilizing everyone in the Navy from 'doing the right thing.' It is the terribly flawed 'affirmative action' policy and process that is at fault, not individuals such as the former CNATRA. The American people must know the facts of this story in order that the Navy be freed of this **campaign of terror** all the

In addition, CNATRA has affirmed to others that the flight instructor involved in the 'fraternization' event had received a letter of reprimand (a career killer) in his official records but The Student Pilot did not receive any punishment. This was an oversight. The squadron commanding officer at the time was transferred during the investigation of the fraternization incident and The Student Pilot's letter of reprimand 'fell through the cracks.' The squadron Executive Officer had not followed through on the administrative details. CNATRA was aware that this had a very bad effect on other flight instructors at the naval air training base.

In the meantime, The Flight Instructors were wondering about the whole process of 'double standards' for the future of naval aviation training. Staff officers had heard The Wing Commander make quite negative vulgar comments about the CNATRA and his decision to attrit The Student Pilot. And they knew of his 'behind the scenes' assistance in The Student Pilot's reclama. So when The Flight Instructors learned of The Wing Commander's public support of CNATRA's decision, they became even further disenchanted with his personal integrity. He obviously had little hesitation to say one thing in private and exactly the opposite in public when it served his purpose.

By the middle of November 1996 (a full six months after the conclusion of the final PRB), the 'informal' IG investigation was finished, and the report completed. The Student Pilot was notified of the decision to attrit her. The Student Pilot was no longer living at the naval aviation training base. She apparently had requested the Navy to send her to Army helicopter training, since she has much obligated service to perform as a result of her prolonged training period.

It is rumored that The Student Pilot has been offered $100,000 for her story by a movie or TV producer. Her attorney reportedly has replied that this is not enough money. The Student Pilot still wanted to fly for the military and feels she was wronged by the Navy at the naval aviation training base. She had not taken any legal action against the Navy, presumably because she needed the Navy's assistance in getting transferred to Army helicopter training. Finally, during January 1997, the Navy simply decided it had had enough. The Student Pilot was transferred to another branch of naval service.

Trust Turns to Terror in Naval Aviation Training

During the entire twenty months that The Student Pilot remained at the naval aviation training base, The Flight Instructors became painfully aware that something insidious had infected their beloved profession -- naval aviation. After the early 'fraternization' incident involving The Student Pilot and the one-way discipline against the male officer invoked by the Navy chain-of-command, they sensed that something was terribly wrong in their Navy. A basic standard of fairness, the bedrock of the bond of trust between its members, was being directly and flagrantly violated. And it was being hushed-up by the Navy chain-of-command so that America would not learn of it.

These loyal young naval officers began inquiring about The Student Pilot's past training history before she had arrived at their naval aviation

---

way up the chain-of-command. They need to know that they can trust the Navy to 'do the right thing' when they send or encourage their sons to serve their country by engaging in naval service.

training base. They found flight instructors at the Navy's primary flight training base, where she had completed her first stages of flight training before reporting to their base. The primary training instructor pilots told them of the pattern of The Student Pilot's previous behavior which had repeated itself at the advanced training base.

Indeed, trust was breaking down between The Flight Instructors and their superior officers. It was becoming clear to The Flight Instructors that their superiors had only their own career interest at heart as they made decisions and took actions that were directly reducing the traditional training and qualification standards of Navy carrier aviation. They knew instinctively that these standards are the bedrock of the foundation of trust among carrier naval aviators. That foundation was being shattered by their superior officers. This was becoming true in the naval aviation training command as it had in fleet operational squadrons where junior officers were observing that[27], *"Junior officers can't trust anyone above the rank of Commander [0-5] in today's Navy."* These junior officers have a phrase to describe their high-ranking 'leaders,' *"...the dark side."* Indeed, trust has broken down in today's Navy.

Terror in the Ranks of The Flight Instructors
As the events played out, as described here, at the advanced training base, The Flight Instructors became extremely frustrated that The Wing Commander was willing to flagrantly violate traditional standards of acceptable performance to pass substandard female and minority naval aviation candidates. But their <u>frustration</u> turned to **abject fear** when The Wing Commander, on more than one occasion, threatened certain flight instructors with a career-ending IG investigation. This investigation would be called if they didn't admit to The Wing Commander an activity that he imagined but of which they were not even aware. The Flight Instructors became fearful that this tyrant could, on a whim, destroy their reputations, their careers, indeed their lives.

There was no person in the U.S. Navy to whom The Flight Instructors could go with their problem. Why? Because they knew The Wing Commander was beyond reproach. As he had often boasted in public, **'I am bullet-proof.'** His record of explicitly and openly championing 'equal opportunity' for women and minorities in naval aviation training made him an icon for the politically correct upper echelons of Navy brass.

The Wing Commander has been observed at social gatherings with mixed male-female participants during which he came very close to 'crossing the line' in his comments to and about women. This activity, if carried out by another, would probably warrant public rebuke in today's gender-sensitive environment. He gets away with this 'innocent kidding' because, in his own words, **'I am bullet-proof.'** Such is the climate in today's politically correct Navy wherein mid-level EEO practitioners carry out the 'affirmative action' policies of their politically correct flag-rank officers. The political cover provided by these high-ranking officers enabled The Wing Commander's brazen social misbehavior. This entire process, overt and covert, of 'affirmative action' gone awry is destroying the U.S. Navy.

One event in this episode turned The Flight Instructors' frustration and worst fears to outright **terror**. When The Wing Commander called for a <u>formal</u> IG investigation on 23 August which involved a training squadron

---

[27] LT _____, Anonymous for obvious reasons, a combat veteran and former flight instructor in the Navy's advanced aviation training command, "Personal interview," 12 May 1996.

commander and a flight instructor for allegedly talking to a reporter, he directly introduced **abject terror** into the lives of all Flight Instructors at the base who had participated in even minor events to ascertain the truth concerning The Student Pilot and let it be known to themselves and their higher command authority.

The Wing Commander, in concert with The Student Pilot, had 'identified' a perpetrator of some perceived violation of the Uniform Code of Military Justice -- based solely on their paranoid speculations. The Wing Commander chose to make an example of one flight instructor solely on the basis that he had been resident at the training base longer than any other flight instructor. This loyal and patriotic young naval officer, completely innocent of any wrongdoing, became the direct victim of the **reign of terror** imposed by The Wing Commander in concert with The Student Pilot and her radical feminist supporters in the civilian community. They would all 'make an example' of this innocent victim.

The Reporter, now in contact with The Flight Instructors at the base, could hear young pre-school children in the background when calling them on the telephone. These officers' wives became very fearful of the direction their lives had taken. The loss of their future, the future welfare of their children, the Navy life that was their livelihood, and their husband's possibility of being subject to a witch hunt, hurled the dagger of fear into their hearts. These patriotic Americans, The Flight Instructors, were forced to hire lawyers or consider doing so.

The Flight Instructors started making calls from pay phones in the event that their home phones were bugged. Paranoia had set in. Fear reigned. Consequently, the lines of communication between them and The Reporter dried up. The **reign of terror** had its effect. Fear and terror invaded the lives of America's young heroes who were only 'doing the right thing.' These young Americans, some of whom risked their lives for their country in the Desert Storm Gulf War, deserved better than this. They can be protected from this tyranny, this **reign of terror**, only if the American people learn of it. America should be extremely alarmed that the heroes who protect them from external threats are treated so outrageously.

Terror at Home, The Relative of a Flight Instructor
At an early date, when the events described here were taking place, a former senior professor at the U.S. Naval Academy (at a civilian academic conference) informed The Author of the identity of a woman who had first-hand knowledge of the 'double standards' then being invoked for women and minorities in naval aviation training. It turned out that this woman was a close family relative (sister[28], wife, or mother) of a young naval aviator who was one of ADM Stanley Arthur's heroes who prided themselves on their role in being 'the first across the beach' in the Gulf Storm War. This young Navy combat pilot was exactly the kind of gung-ho 'warrior' that the Navy, indeed the nation, must retain in order to maintain a first class military.

But this young 'warrior' subsequently had become so disenchanted with what he observed as a flight instructor at the naval aviation training base to which he was assigned that he resigned from active duty. The double

---

28 Take your pick. This artifice is necessary to protect the identity of both The Relative and the former flight instructor. They both fear the long arm of the Navy's **campaign of terror** against them if their identities should become known.

standards at work there for women and minorities was obvious, flagrant, and apparent to all. He became so disgusted with this mess that he gave up his chosen profession, naval aviation. He even turned down an $80,000-plus bonus for 'signing up' for another tour of duty. He resigned.[29,30,31]

This situation was very depressing to this young naval aviator who has a wife and pre-school children. He and they were forced to give up a profession and way-of-life which they all loved. All of this was also very upsetting to The Relative of this young naval officer. She could not believe that the U.S. Navy would treat America's finest in such tawdry fashion. She knew that if her family member spoke out about the double standards that he had observed first-hand while at the naval aviation training base, his career -- the career he dearly loved -- would be summarily terminated.

The Relative also related to The Author an event that had occurred while she had visited her family member at the naval aviation training base. At an Officers' Club celebration, a 'winging,' an outrageous act had taken place. The Wing Commander, in the presence of others, had 'made a pass' at her. Her outrage at this act, perpetrated against her, a happily married relative of the flight instructor under the command of The Wing Commander, was sufficient to galvanize her to action.

After the principled young flight instructor had left active duty, The Relative started organizing a group of 4,000 relatives of military personnel in her part of the country far removed from the naval aviation training base. She visited her Senator, his staff, and editors of local newspapers to tell her family member's story. The Senator and his staff were incredulous at her tale of unfairness and the breakdown of morale in naval aviation training. She provided information to The Author concerning events and people, including her family member, who were directly connected to the events reported here.

Later on, an editor of a major newspaper in The Relative's local area, warned her that her activities could lead to drastic reprisals from naval and other political authorities which could render her family member unemployable in his chosen civilian career. Consequently, The Relative abruptly terminated her quest. The future welfare of her family member and his children could not be sacrificed in the name of 'correcting the wrongs' of naval aviation training. The Relative severed all connection to the

---

29 This phenomenon has become so widespread that the Navy is having great difficulty in retaining 'department head' level aviators to fill the billets that young Lieutenants and Lieutenant Commanders fill in naval aviation squadrons. These young warriors are leaving the Navy in droves. For example, see Blazar, Ernest, "Pilot drain in Navy has Johnson worried," NAVY TIMES, 10 March 1997.
30 This phenomenon is widespread in the other flying services. For example, the U.S. Air Force has the worst pilot shortage, especially in the fighter community, where it is short 837 company-grade fighter pilots. Marine officials have told Congress that pilots are resigning at 'alarmingly high levels.' The Navy, so far in 1997 is retaining only two-thirds of the F/A-18 Hornet pilots it needs and only half the EA-6B pilots it needs. See Bird, Julie, "Bonuses, early retirement eyed for pilots," NAVY TIMES, 7 April 1997.
31 Marine F/A-18 squadrons are now faced with a 10-month turnaround time for deployments. Marine pilots are choosing to 'walk' rather than stay in the Marine Corps. See Pittman, Buster, "Stop whining, and fly your jets," NAVY TIMES, 7 April 1997.

public, her Senator, and The Author. **Fear**, due to the threat of a U.S. Navy **campaign of terror**, would again stifle the truth.

Terror in the Local 'Free' Press

The Reporter in this story is a veteran journalist with over twenty years 'on-the-beat' newspaper experience. The Reporter has verified from over twelve independent sources, all speaking 'off-the-record,' the central events described here.

The fact that The Student Pilot had threatened a lawsuit against The Newspaper, rendered it (under advice of its lawyers) pliable as putty. After lengthy delay and considerable indecision in balancing the public's interest in knowing the truth of a matter that directly affects our national security -- the morale and effectiveness of those 'warriors' who protect us from external threats -- against the privacy interests of The Student Pilot, The Newspaper wilted. After intermediate decisions to delay publication of the story until receiving the FOIA request for the 'informal' IG investigation report, The Newspaper's decision-makers finally decided to not publish the story.

The fact that the U.S. Navy would not honor a FOIA request for the IG investigation report and the fact of the threat of a lengthy and costly law suit gave support to the decision to suppress the story. Freedom of the press, one of the major guarantors of America's experiment with democracy, had been trashed.

The Flight Instructors would be particularly frustrated by this decision. When a very few^{32} naval aviators behave boorishly, as in the Tailhook '91 scandal, it is all over the front pages of the nation's newspapers and on prime time national television programs. But when naval aviators 'do the right thing' and are vindicated by higher naval authority, there is a <u>deafening silence</u>. America would never know of their virtue. Thus, morale took another blow. Terror had prevailed.

A new form of terror would join the **'reign of terror'** invoked within the Navy to suppress the truth. This new form of terror -- legal action by subversive special-interest groups with an agenda to destroy the U.S. military -- is the use of the legal process, the rule of law, to terrorize individuals, the press, and any patriotic American who would get this important story to the American people.

What had precipitated this grave situation -- trust turned to terror in naval aviation training? After all, no one would have anticipated that a simple experiment with women-in-combat would be other than it was logically touted to be. That is, this experiment was to further a woman's right to 'equal opportunity' in the Navy, a right to obtain experience which would lead to careers for women at the highest rank in the U.S. Navy of the 1990s. This 'right' would only logically be balanced by the requirements of military readiness. The high-level Navy leadership would see to this balance. Wrong!

The precursor of this turn to terror was the Navy's invocation of double standards of performance for females and males since the early 1980s.

---

32   Gutmann, Stephanie, "Sex and the Soldier," The New Republic, 24 February 1997. *"Tailhook was officially declared a symptom of a larger problem -- not an isolated event involving <u>at most</u> about six men -- when investigators were ordered to scrutinize the 'cultural' context."*

The gradual 'feminization' of these standards began with the entry of females in the U.S. Naval Academy in 1976 which gradually but inexorably became cemented into naval aviation training by the time of the events of this story -- the mid-1990s. Since the reduction of standards for females would obviously meet resistance by American males, acculturated by American civilization to fair play and competition for the recognition of excellence, the Navy brass would have to invoke extreme measures to enforce this new 'feminization' of naval aviation. As Bill Lind would say in a different context[33], "*When multiculturalism fails, as it always will, the result is 'bayonets.'*" In naval aviation training, the 'bayonet' would be the invocation of terror in the lives of The Flight Instructors who would 'do the right thing' and hold out for even a modicum of a <u>minimum</u> standard. Thus, the activity which precipitated the **reign of terror** described in this story was the introduction of <u>double standards</u> in the Navy, one for females and the other for males. This led to reduced standards for all.

A Summary History of the Reduction of Naval Aviation Standards

The Author first became aware of reduced qualification and training standards in naval aviation when he observed on national television news the fatal accident of LT Kara Hultgreen. She was the first female naval aviator to die while flying a combat aircraft after Congress lifted the ban on women in combat aviation in 1993. This television broadcast showed only the final four seconds of that carrier approach on 25 October 1994. This view of the approach, made in broad daylight, clear weather, and calm seas, revealed only that her aircraft was completely out of control before dramatically crashing into the sea. The Author's past experience as a Landing Signal Officer (LSO)[34] prompted a curiosity to see more of that fatal attempt to land aboard the USS Abraham Lincoln. Consequently, he obtained the flight deck video of LT Hultgreen's last approach, including the last twelve (12) seconds of which revealed that the pilot had induced an engine stall and then failed to implement the proper recovery technique which led to her death and which nearly killed her radar intercept officer (RIO) who ejected them both at the last second. LT Hultgreen had made a 'rookie' mistake and died as a result. She was also responsible for the near-death of her back-seat RIO.

Having seen this video with his own eyes, The Author was incredulous when the then-Chief of Naval Operations (CNO), ADM Jeremy Boorda, and other high-ranking Navy officers went on national television (including Ted Koppel's 'Nightline') and lied to the American people regarding the cause of LT Hultgreen's fatal accident. The Author sent out press releases[35,36,37,38,39,40] and contacted reporters and editors of major national

---

33 Lind, Bill, "The Next Revolution," NET-TV, 10:00 p.m., 30 October 1996.

34 The LSO is an experienced carrier naval aviator who stands at the stern of an aircraft carrier and assists the pilot via radio and light signals during day and night carrier landings. The LSO, after observing and controlling thousands of day and night carrier landings, develops a keen skill of observing trends during the approach that are not yet apparent to the pilot. He can see and sense sink rates, power levels, angle of attack (airspeed) and deck motion <u>long before</u> (fractions of a second) they become apparent to the pilot.

35 Atkinson, Gerald L., "The Hultgreen Affair: The Big Lie," press release, 23 March 1995.

newspapers and TV stations revealing the truth of this matter. The Author's recently published book[41] gives a detailed account of this sequence of events.

Indeed, the cause of LT Hultgreen's fatal accident was pilot error and not engine (mechanical) malfunction as claimed by the Navy brass. This view has been verified by numerous reputable accounts[42,43], including an official U.S. Navy report[44], after the immediate erroneous national media misinformation campaign. The Author conducted a Lexis-Nexis search of major newspapers and found twenty accounts[45] of LT Hultgreen's fatal accident which attributed its cause to engine malfunction and not pilot error. Only one public account even hinted at the true cause -- pilot error. The U.S. Navy's public relations blitz had worked. It deluded Americans into believing the Navy's official spin. There would be no revelation of the fact of double standards, one for males and a reduced standard for females, in naval aviation training, in this case accorded to the first crop of female 'fighter pilots.' LT Hultgreen's death could, indeed, be attributed directly to the fact of this double standard. High-level Navy brass and their political overlords would be culpable.

But LT Hultgreen's fatal accident and its public reporting was not the most important aspect of this episode. It became known that LT Hultgreen and another female naval aviator had been given preference in both their flight training and the beginning of their combat fighter training in the Fleet Replacement Squadron (FRS). They had been placed ahead of an 18-month pipeline of male fighter pilot candidates awaiting such training.[46] A knowledgeable and reputable analyst had received (via a freedom of information act (FOIA) request from the Navy) a copy of the two females'

---

36   Atkinson, Gerald L., "Fatal Error, Lethal Deceit: The consequences of the Navy's Coverup," Defense Media Review, pp. 3, Boston University Defense Journalism, Volume IX, Number 4, April 1995.

37   Atkinson, Gerald L., "The 'McNamara-ization' of the U.S. Navy," News Release, 30 April 1995.

38   Atkinson, Gerald L., "A double standard for female aviators?," The Washington Times, FORUM, 4 June 1995.

39   Atkinson, Gerald L., "Navy breaches integrity at the very highest levels," The San Diego Union-Tribune, 7 July 1995.

40   Atkinson, Gerald L., "Was Command Influence Exerted on LT Hultgreen's MIR?: Endorsements Will Prove High-Level Corruption," News Release, 23 June 1995.

41   Atkinson, Gerald L., 'The New Totalitarians: Bosnia as a Mirror of America's Future,' Atkinson Associates Press, P.O. Box 1417, Clinton, MD 20735, 1996.

42   Vistica, Gregory L., "Fall from Glory: The Men Who Sank the U.S. Navy," Simon & Schuster, 1995.

43   Caldwell, Robert J., "Navy admits 'concessions' for female F-14 pilots: Internal report shed new light on charges of training bias," The San Diego Union-Tribune, 2 March 1997.

44   America Online: Military City Online, keyword MCOHQ, select Libraries, then Text, "F-14A Mishap Investigation Report of LT Kara Hultgreen's fatal accident," week of 20 March 1995.

45   Atkinson, Gerald L., "The Hultgreen Affair: The Big Lie," press release, 23 March 1995.

46   Ibid, Vistica, Gregory L.

flight training records. Therein was ample evidence of a double standard[47] in the F-14A fighter training squadron -- one standard for males and another, lower standard, for females.

The fact of this double standard in the most elite of the U.S. Navy's aviation training units, the FRS squadron, led The Author to look deeper into naval aviation training. He found solid evidence that a double standard not only exists now, but it had begun throughout the entire naval aviation training establishment in the early 1980s. Such a double standard had indeed been building for over 15 years for preferred groups -- minorities and women. Not only had these naval aviation qualification programs adopted double standards for quotaed groups under the aegis of 'affirmative action' but the time-tested standards for white males had been gradually, almost imperceptibly, but absolutely lowered over time. This fact is documented in The Author's book.[48]

That book presents the case of LCDR Stacy Bates, who crashed his F-14A fighter into a suburb of Nashville, TN, as illustrative of this degradation of standards. This supposedly experienced naval aviator was in fact a 'nugget,' a novice naval aviator with fewer than 1,000 pilot hours. He killed himself, his RIO, and three civilians as a result of an unauthorized and faultily executed high-performance steep-angle take-off aimed at 'showing off' before his parents in the vicinity. His flying record was blemished with many flawed performances. As it turns out, he was a member of another preferred group at the time -- naval flight officers (NFOs), back-seaters, who desired to become pilots.

The Author recalls that about 25-30 percent of those who entered flight training with him in 1953 did not receive their 'wings of gold.' A fraction of this 'failed' group dropped on request. That is, they either became airsick while flying or simply realized that they did not enjoy flying as much as they originally thought they would. But at least half of this 25-30 percent were 'washed out' or attrited by their flight instructors. They were simply not aeronautically adapted for flying. They did not possess the requisite mental and physical skills to become naval aviators. Their responses to random emergencies for which they were briefed and which they experienced, under the control of and watchful eye of their flight instructors, revealed that they could not adapt to stressful situations that required sound 'headwork.'

The Author sought out and found Air Force pilots who earned their wings in the mid-1950s time frame. One of these, an Air Defense Command fighter pilot[49], verified that the attrition rate for pilot trainees in his group was around 30-40 percent. Indeed, only the best could make it through the rigorous, stressful process of screening out those who 'could not hack it' in Air Force fighter pilot training. He considered 30-40 percent attrition to be about right since this rigorous training process screened out those who, in spite of their desires, would be hazardous to themselves and to their fellow fighter pilots in a dangerous profession if they were allowed to wear the coveted 'silver wings.' This Air Force fighter pilot introduced The Author to one of the Tuskegee Airmen, the celebrated black American fighter pilots who earned the highest reputation for aviation excellence

---

[47] Donnelly, Elaine, "Special Report: Double Standards in Naval Aviation," The Center for Military Readiness, 25 April 1995.
[48] Atkinson, Gerald L., 'The New Totalitarians: Bosnia as a Mirror of America's Future,' Atkinson Associates Press, P.O. Box 1417, Clinton, MD 20735, 1996.
[49] Himes, J. E., "Private conversation," 5 July 1996.

during World War II. Maybe their success story would tell us something about the importance of high standards in combat aviation.

The Tuskegee Airmen

Lieutenant Colonel Woodrow 'Woody' Crockett, USAF (Retired), is a proud World War II veteran and a member of the famous Tuskegee Airmen. This WWII hero knows first-hand the rigorous screening process that was applied to America's first black combat pilots. He earned his Air Force 'silver wings' under the most stringent scrutiny and rigorous training and qualification standards ever applied to combat aviators. And he knows that this screening process produced one of the world's best combat aviation fighting units.

Many who have read the history of the Tuskegee Airmen may believe that overt white racism was the cause of the stringent training and qualification standards applied to the first black aviation candidates. Indeed, overt white racism was the obstacle that black Americans had to overcome in order to even be eligible for flight training. Overt white racism blocked the opportunity to even try to earn their 'silver wings.' But you may be surprised to learn that racism was not the driving force behind the very high standards required of the first black American airmen. In truth, those standards were set entirely by prescient black flight instructors. But I am getting ahead of the story.

Partially as a result of a 1925 study, "Colored Troops in Combat," which detailed the record of the 9th and 10th Cavalry Division in World War I, the War Department opened the Army artillery to blacks. Crockett, an excellent math student[50], was accepted into the first black artillery unit. He joined the Army in August 1940 and was sent to Fort Sill, OK. This unit was commanded by white Army officers. The Army wanted all college and high school graduates in this unit. Eight volunteers from Arkansas, including himself, were in this unit. Crockett spent two years learning to fire and maintain 155 mm guns. He ended up as a cited 'model soldier' in this unit.

In 1941, the Army started recruiting blacks into aviation. This occurred after Eleanor Roosevelt flew in an open-cockpit trainer with a black flight instructor at Tuskegee and after a Howard University student sued the U.S. Government over the discrimination against blacks in Army aviation. For Crockett, the pay of $245/month compared to $125/month for an artilleryman of the same grade cinched his decision to volunteer for pilot training. He volunteered and went to Tuskegee, AL and joined the twelfth class to enter flight training there.

Crockett waited a year before being called to Tuskegee. During this time he read a book by General Ira Eacker and General Hap Arnold, Chief of the Army Air Corps, which revealed that the Army at that time 'washed out' or attrited[51] "...*75 percent of the aviation cadets they took in overall.*" Consequently, Crockett expected that the training at Tuskegee would be tough -- across the board -- in every aspect of his training. He was not disappointed in this expectation.

Crockett entered flight training one year behind the first class, the class that contained Benjamin O. Davis, Jr., who was to become the U.S. Air

---

[50] Woody's goal was to become a Ph.D. in math by age 25. See Riley, Eddie C., "American heroes Remembered: The Tuskegee Airmen," Sergeants, The Air Force Association, December 1992.
[51] Riley, Eddie C., "American Heroes Remembered: The Tuskegee Airmen," Sergeants, The Air Force Association, December 1992.

Force's first Black Lieutenant General. Crockett's class was designated 43-C, the twelfth class at Tuskegee, which graduated on 25 March 1943. This class started flight training with 35 black aviation candidates. After nine weeks of primary flight training, the final hurdle of which was to solo (fly alone without a flight instructor) for a prescribed number of take-offs and landings, twenty students were 'washed out,' failed. That is, <u>57 percent</u> were attrited after only the first stage of flight training. No second chances. Failure to meet standards meant GONE -- out of there!

When asked whether white racism caused this high attrition rate, LCOL Crockett responds[52], "*No. All of the flight instructors were <u>black</u>. The standards were very tough because these black flight instructors knew that the successful candidates must be 'the best.' They had to show America that blacks could fly as well and fight as courageously as any white aviator.*" Thus, **'Black pride'** fueled the drive to keep the standards high -- not white racism. The black flight instructors did not let any weak flying candidates through. "*They knew that failure later on would embarrass blacks, kill the pilot and maybe others. Consequently, the standards were kept very high by the black flight instructors. They knew the final product must be above average.*" This prescience paid off[53]. Those who eventually graduated performed as well or better in the all-black fighter squadrons as any all-white unit in World War II. High standards produced the best aviation units in aviation history.

Since black flight instructors with formation and gunnery experience did not exist in those days, Crockett's class completed advanced flight training with all-white instructor pilots with one white Major in charge. LCOL Crockett attests that these white flight instructors were all volunteers who were quite fair and displayed no racial bias in their demeanor. They were, however, very tough and as demanding as the black flight instructors in primary flight training. During this final stage of training, two more black student aviators were attrited. Thus, only 13 out of the original 35 black aviation candidates in his class graduated. This <u>63 percent</u> total attrition rate is consistent with other classes graduating at Tuskegee. The table on the next page presents the attrition rate[54] for the first twelve classes of the Tuskegee Airmen.

The very high standards met by the first black American fighter pilots is reflected by the 61 percent overall attrition rate for the first twelve classes. These high standards produced one of the best combat aviation records in World War II. Many may have been called but only a few were privileged to serve. These high standards guaranteed the outstanding combat performance of these superb black American fighter pilots.

LCOL Crockett was the 79th Tuskegee Airman of the 900 to 996 who went through the Tuskegee program. He logged more than 5,000 flight hours and 520 combat flying hours during his career. He flew 107 missions in four months of fighting over the Anzio beachhead in Italy. At the time, 50 missions allowed one to rotate back to the U.S. and out of the combat theater. But LCOL Crockett and his squadron mates refused to be rotated

---

[52] Crockett, Woodrow 'Woody', Lieutenant Colonel, USAF (Retired), "Private telephone conversation," 10 July 1996.
[53] Woody Crockett notes that these attrition rates were consistent with those of the entire Southeast Training Command which encompassed the Tuskegee Airmen and white aviation candidates at other training bases in the Southeast United States. Crockett, Woodrow 'Woody', Lieutenant Colonel, USAF (Retired), "Private telephone conversation," 21 April 1997.
[54] "The Tuskegee Airmen," 18th National Convention, 8-13 August 1989, Tuskegee Airmen, Inc.

Class Number	Initial No. of Students	Number Students Completed	Attrition Rate Percent
1st (SE-42C)	13	5	62
2nd (SE-42D)	13	3	77
3rd (SE-42E)	15	4	73
4th (SE-42F)	35	14	60
5th (SE-42G)	20	8	60
6th (SE-42H)	20	9	55
7th (SE-42I)	20	11	45
8th (SE-42J)	10	4	60
9th (SE-42K)	20	8	60
10th (SE-43A)	15	6	60
11th (SE-43B)	20	7	65
12th (SE-43C)	35	13	63
Totals	**236**	**91**	**61**

because they wanted the 'black aviation experience' to succeed. He flew 149 missions total to help assure this success.

Overall, the Tuskegee Airmen suffered 66 pilots killed in combat; 32 were shot down and became prisoners of war[55]. They destroyed or damaged 409 German aircraft and more than 950 ground transportation units. They sank a destroyer using only machine-gun fire, the only time this was accomplished in this war theater during World War II. They shot 111 German fighters out of the air and, during their bomber escort missions, <u>never lost an escorted bomber to enemy fighters</u>. They became so proficient at escort duty that bomber squadrons explicitly requested escort by the 'Red Tail' all-black fighter unit. LCOL Crockett was one of the Tuskegee Airmen who flew the 24 March 1945 strike on Berlin, where his unit shot down three ME-262 jet fighters while flying the propeller-driven P-51 fighter.

LCOL Woodrow Crockett attributes the success of the Tuskegee Airmen in large part to the rigorous, stringent, and demanding training and qualification standards that they were required to meet before becoming fighter pilots -- one of the world's best. Not only did these standards produce the best fighter pilots, it built a climate of **mutual trust** which engendered superb morale. LCOL Crockett can hardly believe that the U.S.Navy now attrites only about five percent of its carrier naval aviation 'fighter pilot' candidates.

The claim[56] that today's young naval aviation candidates are 'better qualified going in, than ever before,' simply does not wash. This dictum has failed in other education and training enterprises in our nation. When

---

[55] Ibid, pp. 21.
[56] Hamilton, Kelly, COL USAF (Retired), "Women in the Military," MSNBC '@ Issue,' Host Edie Magnus with guests LT Carey Lohrenz, LtCol Rhonda Cornum, and Dr. Gerald L. Atkinson, CDR USN (Retired), 3:00 p.m., 18 March 1997. COL Hamilton asserted that nearly everyone 'passes' in military aviation today because the 'caliber of people going through is very high.' She says, *"We don't take a lot of people into the military anymore. And we are very particular about those who do come through. Therefore we are apt to pick and choose and the caliber of people is extremely high."*

'all who enter' graduate, we find many public high school graduates who cannot read their own diplomas. And when 'all who enter' graduate, we have college graduates who are basic math, science, and engineering-challenged.

More importantly, the Navy has recently revealed that women and minorities are 'washed out', that is, attrited from strike aviation training at a rate <u>four times</u> that of white males. Even those who see the disparity as evidence of bias against females <u>defend</u> the Navy's advanced jet training program. For example, they say that[57] *"Women and minorities entering the program are not of the highest caliber, unlike the white men in the program, because corporate competition woos the best minority and female candidates into better-paying civilian jobs."* Indeed, the caliber of <u>all</u> who 'pass' is **not** 'very high.' The fact is that the Navy's 'affirmative action' policy in naval aviation training has reduced standards for all.

As we shall see, a diminution of training and qualification standards leads downward -- for both morale and fighting effectiveness. This has occurred, over time, in naval aviation. We now have naval aviation candidates and some naval carrier aviators who are aviation-challenged. They are substandard performers. But they graduate anyway. Some of those who do not 'pass' burden the system with charges of 'discrimination.'

The Case of Ltjg Gary Commock

The Author has documented in detail elsewhere[58] the steady degradation of training and qualification standards in naval aviation since the early 1980s. This process has been part of naval aviation training for some time. More recently, there is widespread evidence of special consideration, relaxed performance standards, and outright preference for minorities and women during Navy advanced flight training.

A former Wing Commander[59] of two naval aviation advanced training squadrons in Kingsville, TX recounts the many times he had been pressed by higher authority to pass marginal and/or unqualified student aviators who were in the protected minority or female groups. In his words, he was *"...called into or called by the Admiral's office at least a couple of times a month for not letting the weak ones through."* It was very clear in the conversation that the flight instructors who failed minority or women students, as well as the Wing Commander who supported the judgement of his flight instructors, could be replaced or given bland evaluation reports if **their** performance did not improve. The minority and female students had to be passed. High-level pressure was applied all the way down the chain of command. Minorities and females could not fail. Some of the few 'affirmative action' candidates who were 'washed out' of the aviation training process filed civil rights suits, formally claiming discrimination.

It is now nearly impossible to weed out marginal or below-standard naval aviation 'affirmative action' candidates. The pressures against maintaining the exacting standards of naval carrier aviation arise from the politics of Flag-rank naval officers from above, the constant intercession by Equal Opportunity Officials [Commissars] in the middle on behalf of those

---

[57] Heines, Vivienne, "A Striking Difference: Is Navy combat jet training fair to women and blacks?," pp. 12, NAVY TIMES, 10 March 1997.
[58] Atkinson, Gerald L., 'The New Totalitarians: Bosnia as a Mirror of America's Future,' Atkinson Associates Press, P.O. Box 1417, Clinton, MD 20735, 1996.
[59] Rauch, Kenneth N., 'Dutch,' Captain USN (retired), "Private conversation," 9 April 1996.

with 'discrimination' or 'sexual harassment' complaints, and the threat of the candidate filing a 'discrimination' or 'sexual harassment' complaint from below. A most flagrant public example of a minority candidate who did not meet the exacting standards of naval aviation training but who still tried to 'beat the system' by claiming 'discrimination,' is that of Ltjg Gary Commock.

Commock, 30 years of age, was dropped from the advanced jet training program at Naval Air Station Kingsville during the summer of 1994. According to internal Navy documents[60] obtained by the Corpus Christi Caller-Times, Commock was given a fair chance and failed. *"Ltjg Commock was simply unable to perform adequately in the cockpit and unable to meet the minimum naval aviation training standards. Ltjg Commock has demonstrated consistently below-average performance since his transition to the strike community [TA-4J jets] and was attrited solely for substandard performance."*

Commock filed a civil rights claim against the Navy. His formal complaint was drawn up by an attorney from the Government Accountability Project in Washington, D.C. He claimed he was forced out of the flight program for reporting racist comments made to him and other blacks, and contested the decision to drop him from flight training. He also filed complaints against military officials, alleging failure to take immediate remedial action, failure to conduct an impartial investigation of his complaint, and retaliation (in the form of attriting him out of the flight program).

Navy officials acknowledge that Commock was subjected to racist comments, but they said neither his race nor his whistleblowing activities led to his expulsion from the strenuous strike jet program, considered one of the most elite in naval aviation. The reason he was ousted, they said, was his substandard performance[61]. CAPT Charles W. Nesby, a black aviator and former squadron commander at NAS Kingsville who had direct and personal contact with Commock's flying record, said in an interview with the Caller-Times, *"In my professional and personal opinion, Gary Commock's race is not at issue. When we talk about his ability to fly a tactical jet aircraft, he just doesn't have the right stuff...Gary Commock is not strike-carrier-aviation jet pilot material."* Later, in testimony before a court-martial of Commock on unrelated charges of defrauding the U.S. Government, CAPT Nesby testified[62] *"I like Gary. I think he's a good person. In my opinion, though, I think he has some deficiencies he needs to work on in his character."* When asked by the prosecuting attorney, *"Is truthfulness one of them?,"* CAPT Nesby replied, *"Yes. I would not be comfortable if my son or daughter -- or anyone else's son or daughter -- served under his command. Nor would I serve with him in combat."*

Commock, who grew up in London, England, says he did not know racial discrimination until his Jamaican-born parents moved to the United States when he was 12. And he says he was not personally subjected to discrimination until he came to NAS Kingsville. Vivienne Heines of the

---

60 Heines, Vivienne, "Black aviation student wants reinstatement into jet training program: Navy officials say he lacks 'the right stuff,'" The Corpus Christi Caller-Times, 5 February 1995. 'This black aviator attrited at NAS Kingsville, Texas filed a civil rights claim against the Navy. He was later court martialled for criminal activity associated with his basic allowance for quarters.'
61 Ibid.
62 Heines, Vivienne, "Commock convicted of fraud," The Corpus Christi Caller-Times, 11 August 1995.

Caller-Times reminds[63] us that "*Although Navy Secretary John Dalton has vowed to increase the number of minorities in the officer ranks, the faces in naval aviation remain overwhelmingly white and male. Nine of the 897 aviators qualified to fly F/A-18s, the Navy's premier strike fighter, are black.*"

Indeed, Navy documents indicate that black aviators were subjected to remarks, that could be perceived by some as racist, at NAS Kingsville during Commock's training. During an all-student meeting in the Fall of 1994, CAPT Steven L. Counts responded[64] to a question from a black student with, "*Are you black because you're full of (expletive), or are you just full of (expletive)?*" The remark was acknowledged by Counts, then-commodore of Training Air Wing Two. He explained that it was "*...a good-humored, intentionally preposterous comment that was not racially motivated.*" Counts later was forced to undergo 'racial sensitivity counseling.'

In another incident, a white flight instructor who was getting a ride home from a bar with Commock and two other black officers reportedly used a racial epithet in referring to his black companions. Another incident tells more about the relations between 'affirmative action' naval aviation candidates and their white male counterparts than is realized in its reporting. A white student wrote this message[65] on a chalkboard in the VT-21 squadron ready room: "**If they have lowered the standards for women and minorities in the cockpit, why should we risk our lives for them?**" As this message indicates, there is obviously something going on at the root level in the Navy's 'affirmative action' program in naval aviation that is very corrosive. This is not the foundation on which **mutual trust** is built. The glue that binds is failing due to the Navy's 'affirmative action' policies.

Several other facts concerning the Commock episode are of interest. It is reported[66] that "*He [Commock] and other minority flight students say they faced a persistent perception that their presence in naval aviation is due to quotas.*" This is always a problem with 'affirmative action' programs. The gifted and talented, as well as the solid average performer, are led to suspect that even they are there as the result of a 'quota' imposed for their group. It is simply a fact of life that a stigma exists when below-standard performers of a protected group are passed through. It exists in the minds of the outstanding-to-average minority candidates as well as the minds of those in the non-protected groups. It is an insidious and debilitating element of the Navy's 'affirmative action' program.

When black naval aviators such as CAPT Nesby, now commander of Training Air Wing Two at NAS Kingsville, are quoted as saying[67], "*In the three years I was there at Kinsgville [in a previous tour], <u>we got every minority through the program</u>. More minorities have graduated from naval aviation flight training...than ever before, and those numbers continue to increase,*" there is a problem. In spite of his claim that "*...we have not lowered the standards. We have not lowered the requirements one iota,*" these denials lend credence to the fact of the existence of lowered standards. These

---

63 Heines, Vivienne, "Black aviation student wants reinstatement into jet training program: Navy officials say he lacks 'the right stuff,'" The Corpus Christi Caller-Times, 5 February 1995.
64 Ibid.
65 Ibid.
66 Ibid.
67 Ibid.

statements subtly reveal the political pressure from above, and a mind-set of those in the middle who eventually judge naval aviation candidates, to give special consideration, remedial action, and outright favoritism for the 'protected groups.' This fact of life is revealed by the comments[68] of Commock's flight instructors. *"...[Commock] was a marginal pilot who was given many chances to catch up with his classmates,"* and *"...a weak student who was showing slow progress,"* and even more telling *"...Commock was below standards but [I] was **directed** to pass him on to the advanced jet pipeline to give him a shot at his wings."* In an even more telling comment on the special considerations now being given marginal 'affirmative action' naval aviation candidates, one flight instructor revealed (in official Navy documents) that *"[His supervisor] urged him to **develop a plan** by which we are going to get Ltjg Commock through and earn his wings."* Indeed, the lowering of qualification and training standards is rampant in naval aviation training.

ADM Stanley Arthur, USN (Retired), gave a speech[69] before the Defense Forum Foundation at the Rayburn House Office Building on 31 May 1996. In the question and answer session that followed, a question was asked that bears directly on the Navy's reduced standards in naval aviation and the reason for the rash of apparently unexplainable safety-of-flight[70] 'stand downs' for fleet squadrons during early 1996. The question was, "In the old days it was recognized that some people could be competent naval officers and still not be good enough to fly the Navy's advanced aircraft. It was not a mark of 'failure' to be washed out (attrited) from the Navy's flight training program. The standards were such that at least 25 percent or so were expected to be attrited. Now, it seems, that the Fleet Replacement Squadrons (FRS), basic and advanced flight schools have reduced standards to the extent that everyone who enters gets passed through. Extra instruction, second, third and seventh chances are given to meet performance qualifications, until the 'below standard' flight students are eventually 'passed.' Whereas it used to be OK to attrit, now the Navy just passes them through the training pipeline and hopes for the best."

ADM Arthur, now retired, gave a forthright answer that reveals the heart of the Navy's systemic problem. *"The answer is cost. It is simply too expensive to attrit a student aviator. So we give re-flys, re-stages, re-everything in order to get **all** of them through to get their wings. It used to be that a student aviator would solo on his 13th or 19th flight, after about one month or so into his training. Now they solo at five months. By this time the Navy has such a huge investment in the student aviator that pressures are brought to bear to get him or her through. This is simply today's high-cost environment."* This explanation, though factual, is psychological cover for the fact that a pervasive 'affirmative action' environment, which has existed for at least 15 years in naval aviation training, resulted in giving, over time, special treatment to minorities, women, and other preferred groups (such as naval flight officers[71]).

---

68 Ibid.
69 Arthur, Stanley, ADM USN (retired), "Demilitarization of the Military, Part II," Speech before the Defense Forum Foundation, The Rayburn House Office Building, 31 May 1996.
70 Garrison, Becky, "Grounded over the Pacific," The NAVY TIMES, 11 March 1996.
71 Ibid, Atkinson, Gerald L., "The New Totalitarians: Bosnia as a Mirror of America's Future," Atkinson Associates Press, 1996. *Preferential treatment was given to NFOs due to a quirk of fate wherein a former Secretary of the Navy, himself a naval reserve NFO, promoted a program of letting 'back seaters,' who were initially*

Granting preferred status to certain groups was already implicitly in place (the early 1980s) long before 'cost' became an overriding problem.

ADM Arthur's argument simply verifies that gradually, over time, standards were reduced to get **all** 'marginal' and 'below standard' aviators in the training pipeline through to completion and their coveted golden wings. Including **white male naval aviators**. This resulted in enough 'below standard' aviators in fleet squadrons that fatal accidents have occurred in the early 1990s that render an uncomprehending Navy leadership without a clue as to their systemic problem. They truly believe the problem is 'cost,' when in reality the problem is the escalation of 'reduced standards' to **all**; from minorities, women, naval flight officers, to some white male student aviators. The new-age solution to such incomprehension is a series of safety-of-flight 'stand downs' with the accompanying psychobabble of discussions of 'how they feel' during 'sensitivity' training.

A fact hidden in Ltjg Commock's case is that he was a marginal 'affirmative action' candidate from the beginning. Besides being a first-generation immigrant U.S. citizen (who fits President Clinton's 'lets look like America' ideal), he is a former Marine enlisted man who joined up at age 18. His prior enlisted time was as an <u>inactive</u> reserve[72] (verified through his service record). The only active-duty time he spent was in boot camp. He also claimed, in conversations with his flight instructors, to be a RECON Marine, a diver, and numerous other things. According to these flight instructors, Ltjg Commock was a liar and did anything to make himself look good or to help his cause in getting through advanced flight training. He was in flight training only as a result of the pulling of strings behind the scenes by 'equal opportunity' conscious mid-level naval officers to whom he was related and by EEO milicrats in the naval aviation training command.

To his credit, Ltjg Commock progressed through Officer Candidate School after attending night school on his own initiative to earn his college degree. While these are laudatory accomplishments, the fundamental question is, 'Why, in the current period of military downsizing, is it necessary to recruit combat aviation candidates from a candidate pool so low on the totem-pole of America's potential? Are we so hard up for naval aviation candidates that the more competitive candidates cannot be recruited from NROTC, the naval academy, or other prime sources?

The answer is obvious. **The U.S. Navy is not recruiting the 'best candidates possible'** to provide for the common defense. It is being used for 'social engineering' experiments involving 'affirmative action' programs that have political, not military goals. The U.S. Navy will not address its 'systemic' problem, from the top on down, until it recognizes that 'affirmative action' is leading it to its ultimate fate -- destruction. A chaotic destruction is being orchestrated by radical feminist[73] special-interest groups and their allies in the Clinton

---

disqualified for one reason or another for the Navy pilot program, have a chance to enter flight training to become pilots.

72 Anonymous flight instructor at the advanced training base.

73 Ibid, Bork, Robert H., *"Radical feminism is the most destructive and fanatical movement to come down to us from the Sixties. Totalitarian in spirit, it is deeply antagonistic to traditional Western culture ... Given its aspiration to remake humanity, radical feminism could not be anything but <u>totalitarian</u> in spirit ... Radical feminists ... lack the power and mechanism of the state to enforce their <u>control over thoughts</u> as well as behavior ... [but] the movement is gradually*

administration, Congress, and the mass media. They are aided and abetted by Republican politicians, including many conservatives, who openly court the female vote by 'feminizing[74]' their political conventions and by their legislative activities while in office.

Navy Admits 'Affirmative Action' Policy in Naval Aviation Training

A recent series of articles in the NAVY TIMES, an authoritative weekly newspaper on naval affairs, admits that the U.S. Navy developed a policy aimed at promoting minorities into combat jet training[75]. According to the Navy, this policy was <u>never put in writing</u> and was applied <u>only</u> to minorities, not women. In fact, however, it was invoked for **both** minorities **and** women in naval aviation training. Two training wing commanders have said that there were some minority students placed into jet training under its guidelines. The affirmative action policy was designed by the former chief of naval air training, RADM William B. Hayden, who retired in December 1996. Hayden, who headed the training command from 1993-1996, said in an interview that the policy was "...*designed to get more minority students into combat jet training.*" Hayden denied that this policy was applied to women. Flight instructors under his command disagree. They say that[76] "*Affirmative action (for women and minorities) has lowered the standards, has set double standards and has hurt the Navy.*"

Hayden said he personally explained[77] the policy to instructor pilots during their week-long Flight Instructor Training course. This explanation, given to new flight instructors <u>verbally</u>, left no paper trail of a policy that would cause controversy if revealed to the public. America would not stand for such a discriminatory policy in the U.S. military, an organization that has been heralded by conservatives and liberals alike for its freedom from discrimination on the basis of gender or race. Such policies would be viewed as anti-American.

Under the Navy's veiled 'affirmative action' policy, minority students who made the so-called 'jet cut,' those with grades just barely high enough to be eligible for strike training, were <u>automatically</u> put into the combat program. That is counter to normal policy, since making the cut is not an automatic ticket to jet training.[78] "*Since most students want to fly jets,*

---

gaining that coercive power in both <u>private</u> and <u>public</u> institutions ... Feminists are revising and radicalizing textbooks and curricula in the humanities and social sciences [of our universities] ... [They] control what is taught in high schools, and elementary schools as well ... it is in keeping with feminism's revolutionary neo-Marxism that the movement attacks [our] culture ... [with the imposition of] **thought control** *... The <u>military</u> is to be used as a means of <u>reforming society</u> and not as a means of <u>defending our country</u>.*"

74 Yardley, Jonathan, "White House Child's Play," The Washington Post, 21 April 1997.
75 Heines, Vivienne, "Affirmative-action policy grounded due to opposition," NAVY TIMES, pp. 13, 10 March 1997.
76 Anonymous instructor pilot at the naval aviation base where **terror reigned** as is described in this book. Quote is anonymous for obvious reasons. Identification would immediately ruin this naval officer's career.
77 Ibid, Heines, Vivienne, p. 13.
78 Ibid, Heines, Vivienne, p. 13.

the Navy gives preference to the top students in primary [flight] training." Only the best get jets -- that is the Navy's declared policy.

But under the Navy's 'affirmative action' policy[79], *"...if a minority [or female] made the jet cut, he or she was put in even if there were only a few openings. He or she was added to the list of top students."* Thus, less qualified women and minorities were placed ahead of more qualified white males in having the opportunity to enter the jet training pipeline. With more applicants than openings, the Navy was setting it up so that lesser-qualified women and minorities were allowed the opportunity for jet training ahead of better qualified white males. This 'affirmative action' policy is the same quota-based activity that is being struck down by Americans all over the land in voting referenda[80] such as California's Proposition 209. The Navy's 'affirmative action' policy awards preference to certain quotaed groups, in this case women and minorities.

CAPT Charles W. Nesby, Jr., commanding officer of Training Air Wing Two at NAS Kingsville, TX, recently said[81] *"...fewer than five student pilots were advanced to the jet program under the policy."* Nesby, who is black, said he favored the policy because it enables minorities [and women] to advance to top leadership positions in the Navy. He was the only minority in his class who graduated from the Navy's Aviation Officer Candidate School in October 1973. According to Nesby, *"In naval aviation, we want to have people given the opportunity to compete for flag (admiral rank). Where do 90 percent of our flag officers come from? Strike carrier aviation."* There you have it. Right out of the politically correct radical feminist agenda for the U.S. Navy and, in time, the entire U.S. military. It could not be stated more clearly and more directly. **Quotas** are being enforced for career advantage in the U.S. Navy.

A former wing commander at NAS Kingsville from 1991 to 1993, CAPT Kenneth 'Dutch' Rauch, attests that such an 'affirmative action' policy was, indeed, invoked in naval aviation jet training. Rauch states[82] that *"...The [flight] instructor knows there are people being brought in with substandard scores. And he knows that the quality of his profession is now being diluted...[their attitude is] 'Why did I have to bust my butt, get all the entry requirements, go through the syllabus, meet the standards -- and now we're bringing in people who don't meet these standards?'"*

The 'affirmative action' policy was among several ways that Navy officials have attempted to deal with the issue of higher failure rates for minorities. The Navy's previous success with remedial training programs for minorities who could not swim gave credence to the same approach for other aspects of flight training. The Navy[83] *"...also started an academic remediation program open to all students that helped candidates who may not have had the necessary technical and engineering background,"* CAPT Nesby

---

79 Ibid, Heines, Vivienne, p. 13.
80 Also the 1995 decision of the Regents of the University of California to discontinue any special consideration of ethnicity, race, and gender as factors in admission and the Hopwood ruling of the Fifth Circuit Court of Appeals (the Texas Law School ruling). See the Association of American Universities statement, "On the Importance of Diversity in University Admissions," The New York Times, 24 April 1997.
81 Ibid, Heines, Vivienne, p. 13.
82 Ibid, Heines, Vivienne, p. 13.
83 Ibid, Heines, Vivienne, p. 13.

says. This step, in a Navy that is increasingly dependent on high-technology in its weapon systems, guarantees that naval aviators will be completely unprepared to perform 'oversight' of civilian contractors and other important engineering billets later in their careers[84].

Observe that this process was the same as that which the U.S. Naval Academy invoked[85] for substandard academic students who could not handle the rigorous engineering (especially electrical engineering) requirements at Annapolis. By introducing remedial engineering and mathematics courses, over time the remedial courses became accredited toward the course requirement. Some of these remedial courses became no more than memorization of engineering 'definitions of terms' rather than a demonstration of how these entities function and inter-relate in the design and operation of a weapon system. Standards were lowered. Students graduated without a proper foundation in the engineering discipline so necessary to both flight training and a naval career. It appears that naval aviation training has fallen into the same trap.

While such remedial programs may help minorities enter naval aviation training, some observers[86] *"...have expressed concern that such practices could allow unqualified students to become pilots."* In fact, we have seen this come to pass in fatal accidents and Field Naval Aviation Evaluation Boards (FNAEBs) in fleet operational squadrons. For example, the cases of LCDR Stacy Bates, LT Kara Hultgreen, LT Carey Dunai Lohrenz, and three other 'failed' female fighter pilots deployed aboard the USS Abraham Lincoln, illustrates the results of 'winging' those at the lower rung of flying competence. Two other carrier pilots, one female and one male, also 'failed,' they were FNAEBed, during their deployment on the USS Eisenhower.

Five of the eleven female carrier pilots aboard the USS Abraham Lincoln either died of their own hand (made a rookie mistake), were given FNAEBs, turned in their wings, or were transferred out of carrier aviation. In

---

84   Anonymous, "Private conversations," 16 August 1996 and 18 March 1997. Source is a former naval officer, pilot, and civilian engineering manager in a Systems Command. He has over 53 years of such experience. He has hands-on experience, both technical and managerial, in systems engineering positions with very sensitive highly-classified programs. He has witnessed, first-hand, the qualifications of female military officers, both Navy and Air Force, in technically demanding jobs. These female officers had only 'liberal arts' degrees and were so unprepared and technically useless that they just 'sat in their chairs' during their assignment to billets which demanded technical competence and understanding. These female officers were attempting to function in jobs that required engineering preparation and where engineering judgements and decisions were required. They were so incapable of making these judgements and decisions that their 'node' in an extremely sensitive and vital function related to attack warning during the Gulf War had to be completely bypassed, absent their contribution. They were useless. One female Navy Lieutenant was a Naval Academy graduate, one Navy Lieutenant Commander was an ROTC liberal arts graduate, and another was an Air Force Captain with no technical or engineering background. Their abject failure is directly attributable to the 'lack of engineering training' and the failed practice of 'remedial' technical training in their backgrounds. Indeed, the training standards have been lowered across the board in the U.S. Navy.
85   Atkinson, Gerald L., 'The New Totalitarians: Bosnia as a Mirror of America's Future,' Atkinson Associates Press, P.O. Box 1417, Clinton, MD 20735, 1996.
86   Heines, Vivienne, "Affirmative-action policy grounded due to opposition," NAVY TIMES, pp. 13, 10 March 1997.

fact, the five 'failed' female combat pilots were the total complement of females on the USS Abraham Lincoln who were trained in combat aircraft. The other six were either helicopter pilots or mail-delivery pilots flying the C2 prop-driven cargo aircraft. Thus, 100% of this first crop of female combat-trained pilots failed. None of the five are now flying aboard carriers[87]. This 100 percent attrition rate, after graduating from the fighter FRS, on an initial deployment is unheard of. The two male pilots who were either killed in a 'pilot error' accident or FNAEBed were also members of a 'politically' favored group, naval flight officers, who could not make the cut the first time around and who qualified under the reduced standards invoked later in naval aviation training. But the carrier deck is an equal opportunity killer. It weeds out those who are unqualified and/or unprepared. Nature took its toll. 'Affirmative action' could not prevail over nature.

Lino A. Graglia, professor of constitutional law at the University of Texas at Austin and an expert on affirmative action, said[88] "...*this kind of affirmative action policy is doomed from the start because it is an attempt to camouflage or evade the fact that the preferred [candidates] are not fully qualified for the program...And since they're not fully qualified...they almost universally do not do as well.*" Further, he identifies an added problem with this practice. "*If entrance requirements are different for each group, it can foster resentment from fellow students or instructors...It creates an official labeling of these groups as inferior, which is perhaps its most harmful result.*"

The Navy's 'Inadvertent' Admission of Reduced Standards in Fleet Replacement Squadron Training

The Center for Military Readiness wrote a letter[89] on 16 January 1995 to the Senate Armed Services Committee. The letter said that the Navy had provided special treatment to LT Kara Hultgreen and LT Carey Dunai Lohrenz during their FRS training in the F-14 Tomcat jet fighter. Through a freedom of information act request, Elaine Donnelly, the President of the Center, had obtained the FRS training records of both female naval aviators. She made those training records public so that the American people could learn of the 'preferential treatment' being given females in naval aviation training.

LT Lohrenz has filed suit for libel and invasion of privacy against Donnelly, The Washington Times, and the San Diego Union-Tribune newspapers. The civil suit concerns Mrs. Donnelly's release of LT Lohrenz's training records (under the identifier, Pilot B, in an effort to preserve the confidentiality of LT Lohrenz) in 1995 while the pilot was assigned to the USS Abraham Lincoln and newspaper articles based on Donnelly's report about LT Lohrenz.

Since that time, it has been revealed that a special Navy report[90], written by RADM Lyle G. Bien, was promulgated within the Navy in January

---

[87] Thomas, Evan and Vistica, Gregory L., "Falling Out of the Sky," pp. 26, NEWSWEEK, 17 March 1997.
[88] Ibid, Heines, Vivienne, p. 13.
[89] Scarborough, Rowan, "Navy says female pilots got extra help," The Washington Times, 24 February 1997.
[90] Bien, Lyle G., RADM USN, "Preliminary inquiry into the circumstances connected with the allegation that standards used to qualify naval aviators for assignment to operational

1995. This report revealed RADM Bien's investigation of the matter of whether or not double standards were utilized in the FRS training of LTs Hultgreen and Lohrenz. The report is a waffle-worded concession that "...[LT Lohrenz] received '*unprecedented*' and '*unusual*' aid, although the help was 'generous but reasonable." In the face of this evidence, however, the report stated unequivocally that "...*[the two female pilots] ultimately met the same standards as their male counterparts.*"

This latter assertion is belied by RADM Bien's supplementary report[91] of 4 May 1995. In this report, RADM Bien nit-picks Donnelly's original claim that "...*[one of the female pilots] had the lowest night carrier qualification grades in VF-24 [the RPS] history.*" In support of his reclama to Donnelly, RADM Bien states that "...*one [male] F-18 pilot made 11 night passes and failed to touch the deck, and one LSO also described the poorer performance of a male F-14 pilot [than the female pilots] he personally waved*[92]..." He further states that "...*some small number of [male] F-14 pilots have been allowed <u>three</u> attempts [the females were allowed <u>two</u> attempts] at qualification at the carrier...*" For goodness sake, if anyone fails to touch the deck after 11 passes at night, and it takes three attempts at carrier qualification to finally succeed, there is a serious problem of incompetence in naval aviation. It is simply incomprehensible that the Navy would even consider passing such obviously 'flawed' male naval aviators on to a fleet operational squadron. But there you have it. While nit-picking Donnelly's pronouncements, and in intended refutation of the fact that 'the Navy has shown preferences toward female pilots,' RADM Bien admits that the Navy has <u>passed substandard male aviators</u> on to fleet squadrons. That is just the point. In any enterprise, when the traditional standards are lowered to accommodate a 'preferred' group, in this case females, the standards are lowered for **all**, including white males.

In addition, RADM Bien turns the role of an instructor pilot or RIO upside down when he describes 'downs' for the flawed female FRS pilots which were **the fault of the instructor**. When one of the female trainees "...*brought her F-14 into the [refueling] pits with the right engine still turning...*" she endangered the lives of both the refueling crews and herself. She was given a 'Signal of Difficulty' warning about this mistake. But according to RADM Bien, we are to believe that it was the RIO **instructor's fault** for not "...*reminding [the female pilot] to shut down her engine...*"

In another incident, one of the female pilots, who was practicing low-level bombing runs with dummy ammunition, was "...*allowed to repeat significant errors -- errors which might have placed the aircraft in danger had actual bombs been dropped -- without correction until after the flight.*" RADM Bien criticizes the flight instructor's giving the female pilot a 'down.' In his view, the instructor should have immediately corrected the female pilot's error during the flight. It was **the instructor's fault**. Of course, it is not flight instruction if the instructor flys the plane and

---

F-14 Tomcat squadrons from September 1993 until the present varied with gender of the officer in training," Letter from RADM Bien to Commander, Naval Air Force, U.S. Pacific Fleet, 31 January 1995.

91 Bien, Lyle G., "SUPPLEMENTARY REPORT ON AVIATION TRAINING ISSUES," Letter from RADM Bien to VADM R. J. Spane, U.S. Navy, 4 May 1995.

92 'Waved' is a term used by Landing Signal Officers to indicate that they were carrying out LSO duties during the carrier approaches by the aviator. The term is a throw back to the old days when LSOs used large colored 'paddles,' one in each hand, to 'wave' aviators aboard ship, that is assist them during the carrier approach.

makes the required decisions during any flight. The only way an instructor can judge whether or not a student is assimilating the required knowledge and acquiring competent aviation skills is to let that student make the decisions and evaluate the outcome. Of course this is tempered by not letting a student actually place anyone, including the flight crew, in danger. There was no danger involved in this incident.

In an even more telling commentary on the charade of covering up the fact of reduced standards in naval aviation, RADM Bien reveals that one of the female trainees "...*during a tactics flight, specifically asked the instructor RIO for information regarding procedures.*" The whole purpose of these flights is to ascertain whether or not the trainee has studied and knows these procedures by heart[93]. There is no one there to ask when your life is on the line and the enemy has you in his sights. You have to know, instinctively, what to do. That is why the Navy trains, trains, and trains its aviation candidates in the proper procedures. These procedures become instinctive after interminable repetition. But one must at least know what the procedures are **before** the training flight that requires knowledge of them. RADM Bien contemptuously criticizes the flight instructor's response to the female pilot's request, "...*I'm here to evaluate, not give instruction.*" Indeed, the instructor is there to evaluate the student's grasp of the required knowledge and skills. If the student pilot, male or female, is unprepared, it is not the instructor's job to give him or her a 'crib' sheet or 'gouge[94]'. Allowing naval aviation trainees to 'crib' or 'gouge' their way through flight training guarantees that substandard aviators will reach fleet operational squadrons.

Each of these examples, and the Navy's official written response, clearly reveals that the reduction of qualification and training standards has occurred in naval aviation -- at all levels. When 'special consideration' and 'unprecedented and unusual aid' are given to preferred groups such as females and minorities, the traditional standards become eroded for all. This erosion of standards may be gradual and subtle, but it is real. RADM Bien's supplemental report unwittingly reveals the truth in this matter in Fleet Replacement Squadrons. The very same truth has been revealed for fledgling aviation candidates at the naval aviation training base in this story.

The Impact of the Navy's 'Affirmative Action' Policy

According to Navy training records[95], "*Women and blacks fail Navy combat jet pilot training at four times the rate of white men.*" According

---

[93] In fact, it was LT Kara Hultgreen's failure to implement the NATOPS 'BOLD FACE INSTRUCTIONS' for recovery from an engine stall that contributed directly to her death, and near-death of her back-seat RIO. These instructions are briefed before every carrier flight and during squadron training sessions. Why? So that they become 'instinctive' and the pilot can react in time to recover from a hazardous situation.

[94] 'Gouge' is a U.S. Naval Academy term for answers to previously given examination questions. It is passed around to assist midshipmen in studying for examinations. It became corrupted in the Naval Academy cheating scandal in 1992 when 'gouge' consisted of stolen answers to an electrical engineering exam. See Ganter, Jeffrey and Patten, Tom, "A Question of Honor: The Cheating Scandal That Rocked Annapolis and a Midshipman Who Decided to Tell the Truth," pp. 83, Zondervan Publishing House, 1996.

[95] Heines, Vivienne, "A Striking Difference: Is Navy combat jet training fair to women and blacks?" NAVY TIMES, pp. 12, 10 March 1997.

to the statistics from fiscal year 1993 to 1996, "...*95 percent of white men completed the Navy's two stages of jet training -- intermediate and advanced strike -- while only 80 percent of female students and 81 percent of African-American students passed.*" Information for this analysis was obtained from a Freedom of Information Act request to the office of the Chief of Naval Air Training, which oversees training of Navy and Marine Corps pilots and naval flight officers at naval air stations in Corpus Christi and Kingsville, TX, Meridian, MS, and Pensacola and Milton, FL.

The Navy's answer to all of this is an evasive denial. That is, "*...they don't compare rates of success and attrition -- the Navy's term for dismissal -- by gender or race.*" An aggressive reporter found the answer, however, by a FOIA request of raw Navy flight training data. In 1996, the Navy graduated 183 jet pilots; all but 15 were white men. Only 46 of the 937 students who entered naval aviation training -- 4.9 percent -- were women; 62, or 6.6 percent, were black, and 55, or 5.8 percent were Hispanic, according to the Navy. According to Navy statistics, the number of women seeking pilot training has actually declined slightly -- 46 in 1996 and 1994, and 47 in 1995, compared with 57 in 1993.

The table below provides completion rates for all Navy student pilots for the period 1993-1996.

Category	No. of Students in Strike	Percent of Total	Number Completed	Combat Training Complete	Other Training Complete
Men	1,269	97.2	1,213	95.6%	96%
Women	36	2.8	29	80.6%	94%
Whites	1,230	90.7	1,177	95.7%	95.7%
Blacks	38	2.8	31	81.6%	86%
Hispanics	31	2.3	31	100%	93.6%
Other	57	4.2	54	94.7%	94.3%

The higher failure rates for women and blacks offer new fuel for a debate on whether women and minorities are discriminated against or if they are receiving preferential treatment to enter training. Navy officials and military scholars, asked about the disparity in failure rates, had different opinions about its cause or significance. But even those who see the disparity as evidence of bias against women and minorities defend the training program. Among the responses:[96]
• Women and minorities entering the program are <u>not of the highest caliber</u>, unlike the white men in the program, because corporate competition woos the best minority and female candidates into better-paying civilian jobs
• Standards for entrance are lowered for women and minorities by affirmative action programs, but the standard for completing the program remains the same for all students
• Most white male instructors view women and minorities as products of affirmative action and therefore perceive lower performance from them
• Women and minorities' performance may suffer because they perceive that they are not welcome
• Women and minorities are reluctant to seek support and study help from fellow students
• There are so few women and minorities in the program that a small number of failures causes statistically disproportionate differences.

---

[96] Ibid, Heines, Vivienne, pp. 12.

Radical feminists and their supporters, both inside and outside the U.S. Navy, claim that the naval aviation attrition figures display a discriminatory bias against women and minorities in naval aviation. Others say that naval aviation may not be the most appealing career choice for top female and minority college graduates. *"One of the most basic reasons for higher attrition rates among those groups is that we don't get the same caliber -- all attributes and qualifications considered -- of people as we do among the white male candidates,"* said[97] CAPT Kenneth 'Dutch' Rauch, former wing commander at Training Air Wing Two, NAS Kingsville, TX. *"This may be a bit simplistic, but for the most part, we are recruiting women and other minorities no differently than industry. We've all got to make that quota, got to be politically correct -- and we'll <u>bend the rules</u> to try to <u>achieve those quotas</u>."*

For some, the failure and success rates of women and blacks are seen as evidence that naval air training is working as it should -- and that only qualified pilots are being 'winged.' Other evidence suggests, however, that this is not the case. The saga of The Student Pilot, a failed female naval aviation candidate, reveals that the pressures are such that intimidation, fear, and outright terror have been used in attempts to pass members of a quotaed group. The fact that The Student Pilot was attrited is essentially beside the point. The damage done to morale in the process of making this belated decision has taken its toll. For example, the Navy is finding it difficult to retain enough LTs and LCDRs to fill department head billets[98] in its fleet squadrons. These are the same LTs and LCDRs who have for some time been witnessing first-hand the double standards that are in place in naval aviation training. They are taking a stand and 'voting with their feet' by not returning from their shore-duty tour in the naval aviation training command to sea duty. It is not that they see a better paying future in the airlines.[99] As one former flight instructor[100] told me recently, *"I'm getting out. It just isn't any fun anymore. All of this 'affirmative action' bull---t is just too much to take. The Navy is selling it's soul."*

---

97 Ibid, Heines, Vivienne, pp. 12, "Opinions differ on whether or not bias exists."
98 Blazar, Ernest, "Pilot drain in Navy has Johnson worried," NAVY TIMES, 10 March 1997.
99 Graham, Bradley, "Military Hopes to Curb Exodus of Discontent Pilots," The Washington Post, 9 June 1997. *'Only 26 Navy pilots out of 65 who were offered bonuses last year [1996] to remain on active duty through their 14th year chose to take them.'* The U.S. Air Force is having even greater difficulty in keeping their young 'warriors.' In 1996, it *'experienced a drop from 86 percent to 77 percent in the proportion of pilots staying in the service between their sixth and 11th years, a traditional measure of retention.'* Graham attributes this retention problem to *'...a rise in operational tempo [since the end of the Cold War]'* and *'...inadequate quality of life.'* But these account for only 47 percent of those declining retention. What of the remaining 53 percent? For these one must look at the double standards, favoritism, and 'affirmative action' policies favoring women in today's 'feminized' military.
100 Anonymous former flight instructor at the naval aviation training base where The Student Pilot tested the system. When he leaves the Navy, this loyal American may become non-anonymous, but for now such a course would render him vulnerable to the **reign of terror** described in this story.

The Destruction of Naval Aviation

What is the lesson in all of this? One conclusion, favored by Navy officials, is that the system is working. The Navy is screening out naval aviation candidates who do not meet minimum training and qualification requirements. After all, the system finally weeded out Ltjg Commock and The Student Pilot. All of those FNAEBs weeded out the weak 'nugget' pilots in operational fleet squadrons. Of course, part of that weeding was by death and destruction, including at least one innocent crew-member and more than a few civilian bystanders.

Indeed, one view of the disparity in the strike aviation attrition rates between white males (5%) and women and minorities (about 20%) shows that the initially less qualified candidates were attrited disproportionately as they should have been since they did not meet minimum standards. According to the Navy, these preferred groups would be given 'access' or equal opportunity to earn the coveted Navy 'wings of gold.' But they would have to meet minimum standards of performance in order to be awarded them. If only this were true, it would be a winning argument.

It is undisputed that many minority naval officers are outstanding carrier pilots. ADM Edward J. Hogan, Jr. acclaims that one of the best[101] test pilots at the Naval Air Test Center while he was the Commander there was a black American. Indeed, blacks and other minority naval aviators have performed admirably at the top rung as squadron, air wing, and carrier commanding officers. These outstanding naval aviators are as good as their spiritual American predecessors, the Tuskegee Airmen. This fact is not in dispute.

Nor is there dispute that a vast majority of the Navy's current carrier naval aviators are as outstanding as or better than those who preceded them. Like geniuses in public schools and universities, they excel by simply turning them loose (with a minimum of interference) and letting them 'teach themselves.' They take to flying like a duck takes to water. They are guided rather than instructed. All they need is the proper flying and combat training experience and they become the best carrier aviators. They master the mental and physical skills quickly and are capable of maneuvering their aircraft at the edge of its design envelope -- a necessary characteristic in combat and adverse weather or night flying conditions when operating from aircraft carriers.

What *is* at dispute is the quality of those naval aviators at the bottom of the performance spectrum, those near the other end of the qualification standards. It is abundantly clear that the Navy is now, and has for some time, allowed naval aviation candidates through the gate with lowered minimum standards. These minimum standards have been gradually lowered over time, at least since the early 1980s, such that a substantial number of substandard naval aviation candidates have 'earned' their Navy 'wings of gold.'

Aviation Safety and Reduced Minimum Standards

What is the evidence of lowered minimum standards? After all, one would expect that a systematic lowering of standards would result in higher

---

[101] Hogan, Jr., Edward J., RADM USN (Retired), "Private Conversation," 23 April 1995.

class A, major incident (accident), rates[102] over time. In fact, these incident (accident) rates have been reduced by a factor of ten[103] over the past three decades. This rate over the past few years is:[104]

Fiscal Year	Major Accident Rate Incidents per 100,000 Flight Hours
1992	2.68
1993	2.65
1994	1.68
1995	1.91
1996	2.06

How can reduced training and qualification standards be reconciled with this outstanding safety record?

The fact is that the U.S. Navy has taken great strides in technology innovations which have improved flying safety. The use of sophisticated computer-driven 'realistic' flight simulators, including 3-D terrain visual effects, has provided a means of giving beginning pilots a great deal of 'realistic' experience in the early stages of flight training (and in the fleet squadron replacement air groups) without even leaving the ground. Flying skills are honed in a realistic manner in the safest of all environments -- on the ground.

These and aircraft design innovations (e.g. angled-deck carriers, rocket ejection seats, hands-off-stick computer programmed pitch attitude control on catapult shots, automatic throttle controls, and automatic carrier landing aids, etc.) have made carrier aviation much safer today than in years past. If you don't believe this, talk to some of the early jet pilots who flew aboard straight-deck carriers. These ships had the barricade and barrier as the pilot's only salvation (and that of their on-deck shipmates) from catastrophe resulting from a screwed-up carrier landing or an unlucky hook-skip over the arresting cables.

Given these vast improvements in naval carrier aviation safety, it is valid to ask why the naval carrier aviation major accident rate is not even much lower than it is. But of course naval carrier aviation is still a very hazardous profession. Few other professions tax one's skills to the extent that does bringing a high-performance jet aboard ship at night and/or during inclement weather conditions under calm seas. When combined with a pitching deck in choppy seas, a broad daylight, blue sky landing approach becomes extremely difficult, requiring complete trust and confidence, as well as perfect co-operation between the pilot and the landing signal officer on the stern of the ship. At night and/or bad weather with a pitching deck, you are simply 'rolling the dice' even if you do everything just right.

---

[102] A major, Class A naval aviation incident (accident) is one which results in either a fatality or serious injury, a complete strike of the aircraft, or $1M or more in repair damage to the aircraft.
[103] Spane, Robert J., VADM USN, Commander Naval Air Pacific, "Anatomy of a plane crash: Evaluating, explaining the results of two different Navy investigations," The San Diego Union Tribune, 13 April 1995.
[104] Freeman III, Roland G., RADM USN (Retired), "Private written communication," 17 July 1996.

FNAEBs are the Key to Understanding Reduced Minimum Standards

So, how does the fact of reduced <u>minimum</u> qualification standards reveal itself in this improved flight-safety environment. It shows up in a direct statistic. That is the increased number of Field Naval Aviation Evaluation Boards (FNAEBs, pronounced Feeee-Nabs) convened for fleet aviators in operating squadrons. These boards, convened to assess the reasons for an aviator's substandard and/or unsafe flying performance, should be extremely rare. After all, by the time a pilot reaches a fleet operational squadron, he has gone through and presumably mastered the requirements of many stages of flight training. In addition to his pre-flight, primary, and advanced flight training (about 16-20 months of intensive flying one-on-one with a flight instructor and other trainees), he must progress through familiarization, instruments, tactics and carrier qualification training in the fighter or attack aircraft he will fly in the fleet before being assigned to an operational squadron. By this time he is not supposed to exhibit substandard flying performance. After all, he had supposedly met at least the <u>minimum</u> performance standards at this stage in his flying career. In fact, The Author, has heard of only one FNAEB conducted in any air group in which he served in over 20 years of carrier aviation.

In current-day naval carrier aviation, FNAEBs are epidemic. Of the first crop of female combat-trained pilots to deploy aboard an aircraft carrier, the USS Abraham Lincoln, five of the eleven either died of their own hand (made a 'rookie' mistake), were grounded by FNAEBs, or turned in their wings. This 45% attrition rate at this stage is absolutely unheard of in the annals of naval aviation.

In fact, these five who failed were the <u>total complement</u> of the first 'combat-trained' female pilots to deploy in an operational air wing. The other six female pilots who deployed on the USS Abraham Lincoln were either helicopter or E2/C2 pilots, the latter flying propeller-driven early warning or cargo-on-board delivery aircraft. Consequently, 100% of the first crop of female 'combat-trained' pilots did not make it. Not one is still flying aboard aircraft carriers[105]. This unheard-of record is not only an embarrassment for the Navy, it reveals the true nature of reduced <u>minimum</u> qualification standards in naval aviation. Four FNAEBs were convened during this deployment, three for female aviators and one for a male aviator.

One other female A-6 pilot aboard the USS Eisenhower at the same time was also grounded by a FNAEB[106] as was a substandard male[107] A-6 pilot on this carrier's first deployment with female combat pilots. The male pilot was a former NFO who was 'winged' in a 'preferred group' program that accorded them special treatment. Flight instructors interviewed at the advanced aviation training base could remember his substandard performance in advanced jet training. Many predicted such an outcome.

---

[105] Thomas, Evan and Vistica, Gregory L., "Falling Out of the Sky," NEWSWEEK, pp. 26, 17 March 1997.
[106] Wilson, George C., "Woman pilot cut from deployed wing," The Navy Times, 30 January 1995.
[107] Wilson, George C., "Navy Orders Female Pilot Off Carrier: Review Board Cites Landing Difficulties," The Washington Post, 21 January 1995.

The flying records of LCDR Stacy Bates, LT Kara Hultgreen, LT Carey Dunai Lohrenz, LT Shannon Workman[108], LT Gerald DiLeonardo[109], and the many other substandard male and female naval aviators over the past five years are direct evidence of double standards for 'preferred' groups in naval aviation training and qualification. The events surrounding the cases of Ltjg Commock and The Student Pilot, as described herein, reveal an attitude within the naval aviation training command of reduced standards at a minimum and <u>no standards at all</u> in the extreme interpretation.

The fact that these obviously substandard naval aviation candidates were eventually weeded out is beside the point. The fact is that they made it as far as they did <u>only</u> because of the political climate of 'affirmative action' in today's Navy. The political pressure imposed by civilians from above, and a compliant Navy brass with career-enhancement as a sole driving force, have created pressure that has <u>in fact</u> reduced the <u>minimum</u> training and qualification standards, all in the name of 'equal opportunity.' These 'affirmative action' policies, all verbal and not publicly traceable, but enforced 'privately' and 'subtly' by the command structure are destroying the U.S. Navy. The Navy is being destroyed from within by its own high-ranking officer corp.

The Fact Of 'Affirmative Action' in Naval Aviation Training and the Concomitant Lowering of Minimum Standards for All

Even the self-serving public denials of milicrats in the Navy command structure provide evidence of the chaotic disintegration of naval aviation training. For example, CAPT William Roberson, currently chief of staff at CNATRA, has recently said[110], "...*the standard [in naval aviation training] is like the bar on a high jump. The thing we are not going to do is lower that bar. We will not lower the bar for the sole purpose of making those [attrition] numbers look better. The obligation we have here in the training command is to make sure every aviator in the fleet measures up to the demands that are going to be placed on them in the fleet. Maybe a better question is, 'How do we attract from the [applicant] pool more minorities and more females who are equipped with the aptitude [for flying]?'*" Obviously, these two statements contradict each other in the real-world pressures of 'meeting your quota' for females and minorities. Political pressure from above guarantees that this clash of realities will lower standards. RADM Hayden, the former CNATRA, recently said[111], "*The ['affirmative action'] policy was that if a minority made the jet cut, he or she was put in [for jet training] even if there were only a few openings. He or she was added to the list of top students. But we never dipped [lowered the bar]. That's what we call it, dipping.*"

The assertion that '...*the bar has not been lowered*' and '*we did not dip*' is belied by the record. The fact that such denials are even made at this high command level is ample proof that something indeed has gone awry with the Navy's underground 'affirmative action' policy.

---

108 Ibid, Wilson, George C., "Woman pilot cut from deployed wing.'
109 Ibid, Wilson, George C., "Navy Orders Female Pilot Off Carrier: Review Board Cites Landing Difficulties," The Washington Post, 21 January 1995.
110 Heines, Vivienne, "A Striking Difference: Is Navy combat jet training fair to women and blacks?, pp. 15, NAVY TIMES, 10 March 1997.
111 Heines, Vivienne, "Affirmative-action policy grounded due to opposition," NAVY TIMES, pp. 13, 10 March 1997.

In fact, RADM Hayden's denial is contradicted by actions taken by The Wing Commander and his CSO at the base where The Student Pilot was attacking the system. During the period of hiatus between The Student Pilot's last PRB and CNATRA's final recommendation, the Navy believed that The Student Pilot, presumably backed by WANDAS, might sue the Navy for 'discriminating' against her. In this exercise, in order to quell outside criticism of the Navy by radical feminist activists, The Wing Commander detailed all of the 'special consideration' given The Student Pilot. This myriad of evidence would backfire on him and the Navy. The morale of the instructor pilots, who were aware of the impact of these 'special considerations' on the reduced standards with which they were being forced to comply, took a nose dive.

In order to counter this backlash from The Flight Instructors, the Wing CSO started accumulating documentary <u>evidence of leniency</u> given to <u>white male</u> naval aviation candidates at the training base. This evidence would also protect The Wing Commander from suspicions by CNATRA that he had overly favored women and minorities during his tenure at the base. The Wing CSO verbally detailed these cases of leniency for white males in flight training to various flight instructors who were all riled up at the time over the entire situation with The Student Pilot. The point could now be made, case-by-case, of leniency provided in the past for <u>white male</u> aviation candidates. Presumably, this would challenge the charge <u>within the Navy</u> of 'special treatment' for The Student Pilot. She was only being given the same chances and opportunities as were given white males in the past. This information, of course, would be **damning evidence** of the <u>fact of</u> lowered <u>minimum</u> training and qualification standards in naval aviation training. Here is a mountain of case-by-case evidence of what has occurred, gradually and subtly over time, to reduce the <u>minimum</u> standards for **all** naval aviation candidates, including white males.

'Affirmative action' policies for females and minorities have necessarily introduced reduced standards in training and qualification for quotaed groups. When insufficient numbers qualify under the rigorous standards, the bar is lowered to admit the quotaed number to the chosen few who proudly wear the Navy 'wings of gold.' This lowering is never admitted officially, nor are the rigorous 'written' standards changed. The acceptance of substandard aviators results from 'fudging at the margin' in the subjective judgements of those whose duty it is to 'pass' or 'fail' an aviation candidate. Extra flights are scheduled for those who fail once, twice ... five times to pass a critical milestone. Unofficially excused 'failed' flights, re-flys of difficult tasks, and extraordinary additional flight hours and training time are given to marginal-to-substandard women and minority candidates.

These activities, known only to the flight instructors and other naval officers in the Wing, will never reach the public record. They are, however, along with the public record, ample evidence of 'affirmative action' policies gone terribly awry, over time, in naval aviation. The special treatment that led to reduced standards for women and minorities had infected the whole system. The <u>minimum</u> standards would be lowered for all, including white males at the bottom of the totem pole of combat pilot aptitude. Preference given to politically favored groups had now worked its poison for all[112,113]. The mold had been set that guaranteed fatal accidents

---

112 Observe that this process of lowering standards to a lowest-common-denominator is precisely the same as what has happened over the past 30 years in our nation's public schools, community colleges, and even our universities. This is

and FNAEBs in the fleet for substandard carrier aviators who made it into operational squadrons by virtue of 'affirmative action' policies gone awry.

Even the Famous Blue Angels Are Subject to 'Affirmative Action'

The commander of the Navy's Blue Angels demonstration flight team resigned in May 1996 after citing[114] "...*'personal training difficulties' that he feared were distracting the elite unit.*" CDR Donnie Cochran resigned eight months after he suspended several of the Blue Angels' performances in 1995 because he concluded his flying performance was not adequate and could have threatened other pilots and even members of the public. Cochran, 41 years of age, was the first African-American to join the aerial daredevil team as a pilot and the first to become its leader, in November 1994.

The Navy has[115] "...*boasted about Cochran during his term, in part, Navy officials have said, because they felt he could help recruit blacks to the Navy and in particular to the mostly white ranks of Navy aviators.*" This obvious 'affirmative action' choice "...*suspended the team's performances, and led it back into intensive training, after he became concerned he was not flying at peak performance...The Blue Angels must fly a series of maneuvers in tight sequence, in which, for example, several jets converge on a single point from several directions [at extremely low altitude and at a very high speed]...Before each show, the team chooses local landmarks, or 'marks' to orient themselves...At a show at Oceana Naval Air Station in Virginia Beach [in September 1995], the team had agreed on two runways as their mark. But Cochran missed his mark, causing the other pilots to adjust to his error...*" This caused such consternation in the team members that Cochran terminated the rest of the performance and ordered the team to land its F/A-18 Hornet jets in the middle of the show[116]. This embarrassment was a first in the Blue Angels' history. CDR Cochran subsequently grounded the Blue Angels and cancelled two exhibitions[117] "...*because of concerns about the <u>safety</u> of the team in general -- and <u>its skipper, specifically</u>.*" A Navy official noted[118] that "*This level of flying has to be almost instinctive. You can't be thinking through moves. It's a level of flying attainable by few people.*"

Without disputing CDR Cochran's successes in the Navy (he commanded an F-14 Tomcat fighter squadron and has been selected for promotion to Captain), former Blue Angel team members described him as[119] "...*a solid but not outstanding pilot who was not of the caliber needed to excel in the*

---

documented in detail in many sources and is summarized in my book. See Atkinson, Gerald L., 'The New Totalitarians: Bosnia as a Mirror of America's Future,' Atkinson Associates Press, P.O. Box 1417, Clinton, MD 20735, 1996.

[113] Ibid, Bork, Robert H.

[114] Mintz, John, "Blue Angels Leader Quits After 'Training Difficulties': Flying Team Cancels Performances Through Mid-June," The Washington Post, 29 May 1996.

[115] Ibid.

[116] Press release from Pensacola, FL, "Blue Angels leader quits, citing decline in his flying," The Washington Times, 30 May 1996.

[117] Blazar, Ernest, "Skipper quits Blue Angels: Citing his own troubles, Cochran resigns," NAVY TIMES, 10 June 1996.

[118] Ibid, Mintz, John.

[119] Ibid, Blazar, Ernest.

extraordinary maneuvers for which the team is famous." They suggested that, *"...**race played too large a role** in Cochran's selection as skipper."* CDR Cochran was the first African-American pilot to fly with the Blue Angels during his first tour with the team from 1986-89, and when he returned as the team's leader, he was the first to do that too. According to the NAVY TIMES[120], *"The Navy, which has **long been under pressure to boost the number of minorities in its officer corps and in key, high-visibility roles**, used Cochran."* Former Blue Angel team members, who support increased recruiting of minorities and who have nothing against Cochran, said, *"...they resent Navy leadership for relenting to political pressure and putting Cochran in a job for which he lacked the skills...in this case, the Navy blew it. Now we are paying the price and thank God the cost didn't come in lives."*

It is clear that 'reduced standards' due to 'affirmative action' pressures endangered even the most respected pinnacle of naval aviation -- the Blue Angels. The reduced standards by which special considerations are given to 'preferred groups' is manifest at all levels within the current 'affirmative action' U.S. Navy. The Navy is disintegrating before our very eyes due to the consequences of the cancer of 'affirmative action' and its concomitant lowering of performance standards. Incredibly, a military service that is **chaotically disintegrating from within** is being forced into a rigid explicit racial and gender structure[121] (12/12/5 percentage of minority groups -- Black, Hispanic, and Asian -- plus 20 percent women) that has implicitly, over time, **caused its current decay. While America sleeps!**

Trust Turned to Terror in the U.S. Navy

The disintegration of the U.S. Navy is exemplified in more than statistics of unsatisfactory performance by some of its fledgling aviators. A much more destructive trend has surfaced in the wake of all of this. That is the **loss of trust**. Mutual **trust** is the foundation, the glue that binds all who subject themselves to high risk in dangerous, hazardous professional environments such as carrier naval aviation. In over 22 years of naval aviation service, I have never found a fellow naval aviator who I could not trust with my life, whether he be a flight instructor, division leader, section leader, catapult officer, landing signal officer, or commanding officer. Mutual trust and respect comes from the knowledge that no one could progress through the demanding qualification and training process of naval aviation who did not pass the **personal** and **professional scrutiny** of a flight instructor or other '**protector of the trust**.'

For example, each flight instructor in basic and advanced training used as a criterion for passing a student, *'Would I want him on my wing in a dogfight or other combat action?'* Or even more to the point, *'Would I want him on the LSO platform at night with a pitching deck while I am on final approach and need all the help I can get to make it aboard?'* Or, as an ultimate operational test, *'Would I feel comfortable **flying on his wing** through murky weather at night after I had experienced complete radio/navigation aids failure and he was my only means to a safe approach to visual contact with the carrier?"*

But even more important, the flight instructor probes for a moral absolute in terms of the naval aviation candidates personal honesty. For example, *"Can this person be trusted to face and/or tell the truth -- even*

---

120 Ibid, Blazar, Ernest.
121 Wilson, George, "Bridging the Gap," NAVY TIMES, pp. 12, 17 February 1997.

if its revelation might be self-damaging?" 'Blaming others' for one's own mistakes is simply not tolerated. Whining and excuse-making are not tolerated. There is simply too much at stake to depend on such people. The weak are eventually exposed and weeded out.

Before the advent of 'affirmative action,' flight instructors had the dominant input to decisions of 'who stays' and 'who goes.' Before the advent of 'affirmative action,' every naval aviator could look every other naval aviator in the eye and know that each had passed these tests. The tests were <u>eminently professional</u>, and they were <u>very personal</u>. Mutual **trust** was everywhere. Now, in the advent of 'affirmative action,' and especially its invocation for women-in-combat, **that trust is being destroyed**.

Nearly every evaluation in naval aviation is subjective. Pilots are constantly evaluated. Landing signal officers grade and debrief pilots on their carrier landings after each flight. Executive and commanding officers evaluate grades and comments to determine if there are deficiencies. Some commanding officers will choose to fly with a pilot who may be having problems to help correct them. And it is the judgement of experienced naval aviators that removes a pilot from flight status, for example, as a result of a FNAEB. This describes the **pyramid of trust** that supports the entire enterprise of carrier naval aviation. Without it, naval aviation is a hollow, feeble and shaky 'house of cards.' In the words of Loren Thompson[122], military and policy analyst for the Alexis de Tocqueville Institution in Washington, DC, "*A lot of the power of these training programs rests on the expertise and authority of these instructors. If you start challenging that, then you undermine the value of the program.*" Yes, and the effectiveness of the entire U.S. Navy.

The training of a Navy pilot requires that the trainee develop a 'thick skin' to criticism. This criticism is often personal, direct, harsh, and always brutal to an elevated ego. The proper successful attitude for a 'trainee' is described by a young fighter pilot[123] in a letter to his father. "*It may be of interest to note that [name deleted] is a Naval Academy grad, an institution that teaches that [women] can do no wrong. When [flight instructors] tell me truthfully that I am screwed up, I believe them and try my best to fix the problem. Someone like [name deleted] would never last in naval aviation because as you know you have to develop a thick skin. When you are told you screwed up it is almost always because you did, not because you are being harassed or discriminated against.*" This is an attitude that produces outstanding naval aviators. Without it, the finished product becomes a group of whiners, excuse-makers, sexual-harassment chargers, and discrimination-case law-suit filers. A fighting force cannot be constructed from such rotten fibers.

The Breakdown of Trust in the U.S. Navy

When the evaluation process is invaded by outside political pressure, the system breaks down. When politics prevails, judgements of who stays and who goes is based on who makes the most 'lawyerly' public relations description. But determining who is right is virtually impossible, because flight grades are personal records and subject to privacy laws. They are

---

122 Heines, Vivienne, "A Striking Difference: Is Navy combat jet training fair to women and blacks?," pp. 13, NAVY TIMES, 10 March 1997.
123 LT _____ in a communication to his father, a retired naval aviator, 30 April 1996. Participants are anonymous for obvious reasons. The son is still on active duty.

not made available to the public. But even if they were, they would not reveal the real damage being done to the Navy by its 'affirmative action' policies in naval aviation.

In the meantime, both male and female naval aviators in the first air wing to deploy with female 'combat-trained' pilots said[124] "...*morale among Pacific Fleet aviators is in the trenches.*" The true damage is the **breach of faith** among naval aviators **whose lives depend on mutual trust.** It is the **loss of this trust** that is <u>**destroying the U.S. Navy**</u>. This trust will never be regained as long as 'affirmative action' policies and practices remain; whether applied to minorities, women, or any other 'protected group.'

This loss of trust is illustrated in a tragic event, the suicide of ADM Jeremy Boorda, the former Chief of Naval Operations. This event revealed that trust has broken down in the U.S. Navy from the top to the bottom. ADM Boorda committed suicide as the result of a complete loss of trust and respect of the Navy Officer corps. He lost the trust and respect of the Navy's senior flag officers when he, in essence, 'fired' ADM Stanley Arthur[125] and 'hired' a failed helicopter pilot trainee, LT Rebecca Hansen. He lost the respect and trust of the junior officer naval aviators, the Navy's 'warriors,' when he and his flag-rank representatives went on Ted Koppel's 'Nightline' and other national TV outlets at news conferences in which they lied to the American people about the real cause (pilot error) of LT Kara Hultgreen's fatal accident[126]. ADM Boorda's suicide can be traced directly to these and other related events. There was, indeed, a complete breakdown of trust in the Navy, from top to bottom. The nation's mass media contributed to this situation by trumpeting radical feminist propaganda on 'sexual harassment' of females in the Navy (Tailhook '91) and the concomitant inevitability of women-in-combat.

The Breakdown of Trust at the U.S. Naval Academy

The Author attended a meeting of a group of academics who are fighting for a return to high standards of structure, content, and rigor in America's colleges and universities. At that meeting, I met professors from the U.S. Naval Academy. Upon explaining my concept of the root cause of the Navy's fleet-wide 'stand downs,' they were nodding their heads in affirmation. These professors had accumulated over 48 years of cumulative teaching experience at the Naval Academy. They explained[127] that "...*fully 30 percent of the midshipmen in their classes were not qualified to be in any college, much less the Naval Academy.*" They identified the problem as lowered entrance requirements for minorities, women, and football players. They also related that the presence of these sub-par midshipmen resulted in pressure from their supervisors for leniency. This resulted in diminished academic standards. Of course, the outstanding midshipmen were still there in as many numbers as in previous decades but the middle-to-lower group of academically-challenged midshipmen were dragging the academic standards down

---

[124] Garrison, Becky, "The grounding of morale at Air Wing 11," NAVY TIMES, 18 March 1996.
[125] Boyer, Peter J., "What Killed Admiral Boorda: Admiral Boorda's War," The New Yorker, pp. 68, 16 September 1996.
[126] Atkinson, Gerald L., 'The New Totalitarians: Bosnia as a Mirror of America's Future,' Atkinson Associates Press, P.O. Box 1417, Clinton, MD 20735, 1996.
[127] U.S. Naval Academy Professors who will remain anonymous for obvious reasons, "Lowered Academic Standards at the U.S. Naval Academy," private conversations,
6 April 1996.

in all of the technology classes. The remedial nature of the instruction was of such substandard quality that it subtly reduced the standards of quality instruction in all of their classes. They had to teach to the level of the substandard midshipmen rather than to higher levels.

There is documentary proof of lowered academic standards at the Naval Academy. In 1990, a civilian chairman of the electrical engineering department was relieved of his post in mid-semester because he refused to raise preliminary grades across the board in two electrical engineering courses and refused[128] to raise grading curves 'across the entire [electrical engineering curriculum].' Midshipmen had complained that "...*they are being given too hard a time.*" Many midshipmen were choosing humanities (Poly-Sci QPR High, the rallying cry for those who took political science rather than engineering majors to boost their point averages) rather than the academy's traditional technology majors. The chairman was removed because[129] "...*he refused a directive [from the military authority] to arbitrarily raise grades given by other instructors in three required courses in electrical engineering.*" The military leaders had been concerned that midshipmen were receiving low grades in electrical engineering for some time. "*For the fall 1989 semester, more than 40 percent of midshipmen in three introductory engineering courses received Ds or Fs.*" It is clear that the U.S. Naval Academy has been slowly and subtly but determinedly lowering standards over time at the Navy's premiere source of naval officers. This practice has directly contributed to a **breakdown of trust** at the U.S. Naval Academy. The faculty do not trust the military administrators. The outstanding-to-average midshipmen do not trust the system that reduces standards in order to accommodate substandard but preferred 'affirmative action' groups.

The Mass Media Contribute to the Navy's Breakdown of Trust

The truth is that shrill radical feminist propaganda, inside and outside the Navy, glossed over the truth of LT Hultgreen's unfortunate accident. Georgie Anne Geyer, a nationally syndicated journalist, visited the Abraham Lincoln and reported that[130] "*When [LT Hultgreen] became the Navy's first female carrier fighter pilot -- and then the first one to die in active training -- she unquestionably became the symbol of all the changes taking place here.*" Ms. Geyer then reported several interviews with men and women aboard the Abraham Lincoln which anecdotally sympathize with the feminist agenda of furthering their goal of women-in-combat to enable women to break through the 'glass ceiling' of command opportunities.

Ms. Geyer poisoned the well of honest national debate on the subject of women-in-combat. She labelled those who disagree with her analysis as somehow subhuman in some basic character trait. She reported that[131] "*LT Hultgreen's memory was besmirched when, after her death, some of the 'old school' sent anonymous faxes around impugning her qualifications. It was not until her grieving mother released her test scores, showing she was indeed above average, that the matter was set right.*"

---

128 Weil, Martin and Leff, Lisa, "Naval Academy Relieves Head of Department: Chairman Was Asked to Raise Grades," The Washington Post, 25 February 1990.
129 Mitchell, Brian, "Firing raises old questions about academy's role: Institution again debates 'university' idea at Annapolis," NAVY TIMES, 19 March 1990.
130 Geyer, Georgie Anne, "Aboard a 'gender neutral' carrier," The Washington Times, 22 January 1995.
131 Ibid.

It has been The Author's experience in naval aviation that the people who know best your flying skills are those junior officers who fly with you. They cannot be fooled. If you are below average, unsafe or dangerous in your flying skills, it is immediately apparent to them. If some of these male junior officers reported (via fax) LT Hultgreen's deficiencies, they did so anonymously since the Navy's currently politically sensitive command structure would cut them off at the knees if they told the truth and gave their identity. It is clear that some of this 'truth-telling' is emerging as a result of the current experience with females who have been trained as 'combat' aviators.

For example, LT Shannon Workman, pilot of an EA-6B electronic warfare jet deployed aboard the aircraft carrier Dwight D. Eisenhower, has been removed[132] from flying status midway through a Mediterranean deployment. She was never able to fully master the demanding task of landing on the carrier[133]. LT Workman was the first woman to qualify for carrier combat duty after a ban on such assignments was lifted in 1993. The Navy made the Eisenhower its first combat ship with women aboard, and when the carrier sailed for the Mediterranean Sea in September 1994, LT Workman was one of its eleven female aviators. LT Workman flew missions in the Mediterranean and in the Persian Gulf before the evaluation board was convened in December 1994 expressly to evaluate her flying. "*There was no improvement,*" said[134] a Navy official of the dismissal. "*You expect to see that person get in a groove, but it was a struggle every time -- It's always a pucker factor. But you expect her to get a little more comfortable. She did not.*" There are ten other female aviators on the USS Eisenhower, nick-named 'Mamie' by old-salt sailors of years past and 'Dyke' by others more recently in commemoration of the recent feminization of its crew. Three are F/A-18 fighter pilots, one E-2 Hawkeye (propeller aircraft) pilot, two helicopter pilots, and four naval flight officers.

In a propaganda piece in The Washington Post before the Eisenhower deployed, columnist George C. Wilson wrote[135] glorious prose of the prospect of LT Workman 'breaking the carrier barrier.' "*The gray whale of an airplane came hurtling out of the afternoon sky, its bulbous nose aimed at the steel deck of this aircraft carrier. The next few seconds would tell whether the 115-pound female pilot could bring the 30-ton plane down on the deck for the controlled crash that is a carrier landing.*"

In reality, the EA-6B is one of the easiest jet aircraft to land aboard an aircraft carrier. A more prophetic quotation in Wilson's piece may have been one from LT Workman herself. "*The most unnatural thing is landing on the boat. It's nothing I can take for granted. I really have to work at it. The lineup is the hardest for me. I'm a very average pilot.*" CDR Joseph Flynn, the executive officer of LT Workman's squadron, said he was not at all concerned that she had qualms about carrier landings. "*I'd be scared if she were comfortable around the boat,*" he said[136]. "*Those are the ones who die.*"

---

132 Wilson, George C., "Woman pilot cut from deployed wing," The Navy Times, 30 January 1995.
133 Scarborough, Rowan, "Female pilot not likely to get back aboard," The Washington Times, 23 January 1995.
134 Ibid.
135 Wilson, George C., "Stretching Their Wings: The Navy's Female Aviators Break the Carrier Barrier," The Washington Post, 8 November 1994.
136 Ibid.

I don't know whose Navy CDR Flynn is in but the Navy in which I flew (jet fighters, attack, and reconnaissance aircraft) recognized the 'comfort' achieved by veteran aviators midway during a deployment by challenging them to day carrier landings with the fresnel lens turned off, forcing them to fly the glide path with nothing to help them other than their 'experienced intuition' and 'feel' of 'flying on the glide path' and 'on speed.' This practice built both confidence and 'comfort.' It also developed a keen professionalism.

It is hard to believe that today's naval carrier aviation training has been degraded to the extent that veteran naval aviators are supposed to be 'uncomfortable' during day carrier landings. Night carrier landings are another matter altogether. But day carrier landings, while requiring 100 percent of the pilot's concentration, are supposed to be 'comfortable' for a competent professional naval aviator. If they are not, then that aviator does not belong. And neither does the substandard pilot's commanding and executive officers who accept such attitudes as 'normal' in carrier naval aviation.

It is of interest to note that the Navy's 'full disclosure' of LT Hultgreen's training records to her mother and the mass media was not followed in the case of LT Workman. The U.S. mass media did not report the details of LT Workman's flying difficulties. One must subscribe to respectable and reliable <u>foreign</u> news media, such as the *Sunday Mirror* of London, England to find information that would allow knowledgeable people to make up their own minds on LT Workman's substandard flying performance. That newspaper reported[137] that "*...it sometimes took LT Workman three or more tries to land her EA-6B jet aboard the USS Eisenhower.*" The paper quoted an unnamed source aboard the carrier saying, "*It just reached the point where we decided that if she carried on there was a real danger that there would be a crash.*"

The American people are being propagandized and pertinent information is being censored by the U.S. Navy, the Clinton administration, and the media elites. Any old naval aviator will tell you that a pilot who requires three or more passes before each successful landing aboard the carrier is not qualified to be a carrier aviator. This shortcoming is clear enough that it should have been revealed during training, not midway in a fleet deployment. It is absolutely clear that there has been and is now a double standard for female and male pilots in the new feminized U.S. Navy.

This troubling aspect of obvious favoritism that LT Workman represents for females in the U.S. Navy is being further compounded. The next step was for the Navy's personnel bureau to find a new flying billet for LT Workman. Downsizing has resulted in a scarcity of flying billets in the Navy. Navy personnel leaders had to deny an aviator (a male) already on the waiting list to enable LT Workman to pilot a C-9, a land-based aircraft. The male pilot was picked for the Navy's TAR (Training and Administration of Reserves) program and was awaiting orders to report to his new command, a C-9 squadron. He received a call from the Navy and was told that he had lost his TAR billet to LT Workman. By favoring LT Workman with such an assignment, the politically motivated Navy hammered another nail in the coffin of naval aviation. This double standard of training, assignment, and deployment rotation is becoming the norm in the U.S. Navy. Meanwhile, morale plummets. The glue that binds is softening. The bond of trust is breaking. The Navy becomes a hollow fighting force.

---

[137] Chavez, Linda, "Woes mount for 2-sex military: Pregnant sailors? Crashing pilots? Coed quarters? Haven't we had enough?," USA TODAY, 1 February 1995.

The revelations in this book comprise a damning record for the Navy's 'affirmative action' program for introducing women into combat positions. It is simply a last straw that is breaking the camel's back. 'Affirmative action' programs that were in place since the early-1980s have been made explicit and more pervasive. The U.S. Navy, once a proud and demanding service, is being destroyed by this practice. And it isn't even aware. Or, if aware, the high-level officer corps is too timid to speak out. Their careers are more valuable to them than their Navy. In the words of James Webb[138], a Marine hero of the Vietnam War and former Secretary of the Navy, *"Some are guilty of the ultimate disloyalty: to save or advance their careers, they abandoned the very ideals of their profession in order to curry favor with politicians."*

Terror in the U.S. Navy

The story told here about The Student Pilot is an extreme example of a well-intentioned 'equal opportunity' policy gone terribly awry. As in other parts of our society, the implementation of this policy resulted in excess, that is, an 'affirmative action' policy that was quietly and subtly undertaken to increase the numbers of females and minorities in the U.S. Navy -- at all costs. This led directly to 'preference' for these 'protected' groups.

Terror in Naval Aviation Training

The Navy has essentially admitted to having 'affirmative action' programs in naval aviation training. This admission, although carefully veiled in a very carefully worded 'arms-length' spin, was revealed in an article by Vivienne Heines in NAVY TIMES[139]. This 'affirmative action' policy was admitted publicly in such a way that we are to understand that it was considered but discarded. But that admission is only the tip of the iceberg. That 'discarded policy' is indeed still in place in practice. And that very policy had been in operation quietly and subtly for some time -- administered verbally and not in written directives. In the naval aviation training command, it had been accelerated since 1993 as the new Clinton administration let it be known that all Federal Government agencies, including the military, would 'look like America.' That is, females and minorities would be actively favored. In this positive climate for 'diversity,' that is, 'affirmative action,' in the U.S. Navy, and naval aviation in particular (after the ban on females in combat positions was lifted in 1993) sky-rocketed. But in fact, this acceleration of 'diversity' in naval aviation was only a visible boost to what had become a subtle but strong 'affirmative action' policy since the early 1980s. This trend is well-documented in the book[140], *"The New Totalitarians: Bosnia as a Mirror of America's Future."*

That book provides a detailed account of the radical feminists' manipulation of the democratic process to serve a totalitarian end, that is, the shoe-horning of women into combat positions at all cost. And in that spirit, when the questionable 'affirmative action' practices fail to produce enough female combat pilots, the 'actual' standards in practice are lowered to such a degree that the flight instructors resist. They recognize

---

138 Webb, James H. Jr., "Copy of Original Draft of Speech Given at the 122nd meeting of the U.S. Naval Institute, Annapolis, MD, 25 April 1996.
139 Heines, Vivienne, "Affirmative-action policy grounded due to opposition," NAVY TIMES, pp. 13, 10 March 1997.
140 Atkinson, Gerald L., 'The New Totalitarians: Bosnia as a Mirror of America's Future,' Atkinson Associates Press, P.O. Box 1417, Clinton, MD 20735, 1996.

'dangerous' when they see it. The reaction, as it always is when 'multiculturalism' fails, is bayonets. In this case the dagger of **fear** is directed at these patriots by their politically correct senior officers. A **campaign of terror** is invoked to threaten and intimidate them. This results in a complete **breakdown of trust**. This, in an organization which depends on complete trust among its bonded members, is destroying naval aviation.

The fact that mid-level commanders, e.g. The Wing Commander in the case of The Student Pilot, could and did invoke a **campaign of terror** on the flight instructors in his command to 'pass' an obviously failed naval aviation candidate is proof of an 'affirmative action' policy gone terribly awry. His **campaign of terror** took the problem to a new, higher level. It introduced a new dimension, a terribly destructive dimension, into naval aviation training. The fear that was placed in the hearts of his flight instructors was real, palpable, and deep. It reached into the hearts of their wives, children, and extended families. All were under the wet blanket of fear that threatened to choke off their livelihood, their way-of-life, and their children's future. Any attempt on the part of the flight instructors to uphold even a reasonable <u>minimum</u> standard was rewarded by the threat of an IG investigation, summarily taking their wings, and ending their chosen career. Their trust and faith in their Navy would be summarily executed. They would be cut off at the knees in the pursuit of a profession that they loved, respected, and desired to pursue for life.

It is ironically and sadly true that The Wing Commander in this story is also a 'victim' of the Navy's 'affirmative action' policy in naval aviation. His dedication to 'going the extra mile,' 'giving the benefit of the doubt,' and 'equal opportunity remediation' to the female and minority aviation candidates under his Wing may well have been laudable in a 'perfect' world. But in this case, human frailties (as will always be the case) interfered. If only the previous wing commander had taken the appropriate action when The Student Pilot 'fraternized' with the senior flight instructor, all could have turned out well. If both The Student Pilot and the flight instructor had been equally disciplined, removed from flying status, this story might well have turned out quite differently. But under the extremely politically charged environment of 'feminizing' the U.S. military, this action might well have resulted in that wing commander's dismissal. It surely would have gained unwanted attention from higher authority, an activity that is feared by all Navy commanders with little heart for 'doing the right thing.' The heavy blanket of fear that has covered the Navy over the past six years has led to such timidity at all levels of decision-making in the U.S. Navy.

The Wing Commander was further hindered in this saga by his knowledge of past history when black Americans, who pushed hard for equal opportunity for minorities in military aviation, were summarily brought before medical authorities for 'psychological examinations' as a means of removing them from the military scene. That is probably why The Wing Commander got in trouble with higher authority by countermanding the Wing flight surgeons' 'grounding' of The Student Pilot. He might have believed that he was seeing a repetition of an activity that in the past had been applied to 'keep blacks down,' in this case, applied to a female under his command. His emotionally motivated decision to return The Student Pilot to flying status, while 'grounded' by the flight surgeons, was, in retrospect, the seed of his downfall -- especially as The Student Pilot failed to perform adequately after this obviously flawed decision.

In this case, CNATRA gave The Wing Commander a damaging 'fitness report,' the Navy's evaluation by superior officers of a subordinate's aptitude for higher command positions. Consequently, The Wing Commander is retiring from the Navy, a Navy that he surely loved as much as did those flight instructors whose lives he terrorized over the course of The Student Pilot's tenure in advanced flight training. This is not a perfect world.

Terror at the U.S. Naval Academy

The professors at the U.S. Naval Academy (USNA) who supplied the information on lowered standards there remain invisible. They are deathly afraid that their identification would immediately result in a loss of their means of livelihood. They know of the abrupt dismissal of a professor at the USNA for exposing the status of 'leadership' training there.

The lowering of admission and performance standards at the Naval Academy is having an effect. James Barry, a professor at the Academy for the past seven years, publicly charged that the Navy is adrift and has a broken moral compass. He charged[141] that the problem starts at the Naval Academy which is "...*plagued by a serious morale problem caused by a culture of hypocrisy, favoritism and the covering up of problems.*" Immediately after Barry's criticism appeared in the Washington Post, five current and former midshipmen were charged with taking part in a car-theft ring[142]. On the same day that the car-theft ring was exposed, another midshipman was convicted of selling drugs (LSD) to an undercover police officer and four others pleaded guilty to drug-dealing charges. Nineteen other midshipmen were arrested for using these drugs. All of this came on top of a 1992 cheating scandal wherein up to 134 midshipmen were involved in stealing and/or distributing and using an electrical engineering examination. In addition, a top-ranked midshipman officer was put in the brig in Quantico, VA, accused of sexually harassing[143] four women and threatening one who reported him. Another midshipman was arrested on charges he fondled a toddler while visiting an Annapolis home on leave. All of this criminal chaos breaking about the heads and shoulders of the Navy has its top leadership shaking their heads in disbelief.

It is of interest to note that the honest midshipmen who admitted even a minor peripheral involvement in the 1992 Naval Academy cheating scandal were punished[144]. Others, equally involved, who stonewalled and did not admit guilt, went free. Each group was known to the other. It is clear that midshipmen, observing what actually goes on at the Naval Academy, learn how to 'game' the system. They resent those, such as athletes, minorities, and females who are presumed to get special breaks[145]. Consequently, sexual harassment is a chronic problem at the Naval Academy. The granting of special privileges and reduced standards for these groups has its consequences. Professor Barry, in his scathing criticism of the Naval

---

141 Barry, James F., "Adrift in Annapolis: To Understand Why the Navy's Moral Compass Is Broken, Start at the Naval Academy," The Washington Post, 31 March 1996.
142 Scheets, Gary, "Annapolis caught in new scandal: 5 current, former midshipmen charged with roles in car thefts," The Washington Times, 12 April 1996.
143 Stuckey, Tom, "Cluster of incidents poses query: What's ailing midshipmen?," The Washington Times, 21 April 1996.
144 Gantar, Jeffrey and Patten, Tom, "A Question of Honor: The Cheating Scandal That Rocked Annapolis and a Midshipman Who Decided to Tell the Truth," pp. 114/190, Harper Collins, 1996.
145 Ibid, Thomas, Evan, and Vistica, Gregory L.

Academy's current ethical standards, states[146] "*These wonderful young people [midshipmen] become immersed in an ethically corrupting system -- one so powerful that, at the start of their second year, most of them are confirmed cynics, who routinely violate regulations about clothing, driving, alcohol and sex, plus any other rules they consider superfluous.*"

It is not lost on the conscientious Naval Academy professors who The Author met at an academic conference that Professor Barry was forced out[147] of the U.S. Naval Academy after his courageous attempt to call attention to a growing cancer there.

The abrupt dismissal of Professor Barry for publicly airing his views has invoked terror into the lives of all professors who would criticize the USNA for lowering academic standards in the name of 'affirmative action.' Consequently, they have disappeared from sight, cowering in the face of a **campaign of terror** invoked by Navy administrators. This **terror** runs deep and wide. It even reaches former naval officers in their civilian employment.

The Case of the Mysterious 'Negative' Reference

A mid-level active-duty naval officer was an instructor in a technical discipline at the U.S. Naval Academy. He refused the Administration's order to artificially raise the grades of an academically-challenged group of female and minority midshipmen. After several threatening sessions by the Academy administrators, he stood on principle and refused to 'lower the academic standards.' He was transferred out of his Naval Academy billet to a dead-end job at another naval command, from which he retired as a Commander (O-5).

This former naval officer applied for a teaching position at a small church-run high school in up-state New York. This relatively low-paid position would require his teaching six classes per week. While going through the interview process, he found that some 'negative' reference material had been communicated to the school superintendent via an anonymous phone call.

One of the former naval officer's friends, a positive reference who had been at the USNA at the time of his tenure there, found out during his conversation with the high school authorities that an anonymous person had called (from a 'blocked' non-traceable phone) to volunteer negative information about the candidate's tenure at the USNA. The tenor of the call clearly indicated that the anonymous caller was someone at the academy. The friend could not believe the charges levied by the anonymous caller because the friend knew in detail the circumstances (standing on principle against reduced academic standards) surrounding the anonymous 'charges.' The friend was fortunately able to answer all questions concerning this matter to the satisfaction of the high school authorities. He had stemmed the tide of a back-door **terrorist campaign** to harm the former naval officer and his family (with children of college-age).

The fact is that the long arm of the radical feminists and their sympathizers in the U.S. Navy, even at the U.S. Naval Academy, is being used

---

[146] Barry, James F., "Adrift in Annapolis: To Understand Why the Navy's Moral Compass Is Broken, Start at the Naval Academy," The Washington Post, 31 March 1996.
[147] Barry, James F., "Messenger Overboard: My Losing Battle With the Naval Academy," The Washington Post, 6 April 1997.

to **terrorize** anyone who stands up in opposition to their Neo-Marxist agenda. While America sleeps!

The Navy has gone to great lengths to hide their systemic problem, affirmative action programs gone awry. A high-profile review panel, during early 1997, studied the problems at the U.S. Naval Academy. In spite of evidence since 1987 that something terribly wrong was in evidence there, this panel[148] simply 'whitewashed' the record. Over six months in the latter part of 1996, midshipmen were arrested on charges of drug use, sexual assault, child molestation, and participation in a car theft ring. This record on top of a widespread cheating scandal involving an electrical engineering exam in 1992 in which 134 midshipmen were implicated and 24 eventually were expelled for cheating and lying. And this on top of a 1990 episode wherein midshipmen were allowed to take an electrical engineering exam despite protest from faculty members who said the test was stolen and possibly photocopied. And on top of this, in 1989, a female midshipman was sexually harassed by male classmates who handcuffed her to a urinal. This occurred in the 1987 time frame, as well as reports of racial bias, hazing, unequal justice and the firing of an engineering professor for refusing to change exam grades prompted a congressional hearing, as well as investigations by the office of the naval inspector general, the General Accounting Office and the academy's Board of Visitors. All of this occurred before the 1997 report by the high-level review panel which essentially 'whitewashed' this record.

The review panel attributed[149] the alleged criminal behavior at the academy to "...*changing values and pressures in the world outside Annapolis...It isn't something that's systemically wrong or that [the academy] gets good kids and turns them into bad kids.*" Critics of the panel's early report were dismayed. "*The first systemic flaw is that Navy leadership is unwilling to hold itself accountable,*" said one former USNA instructor. He scoffed[150] at the new panel's contention that societal problems are to blame for the academy's woes. Other critics say that the panel may have overlooked larger, more encompassing problems at the academy.

Exactly! The U.S Naval Academy is only one of the naval entities for which the Navy is overlooking completely its major systemic problem -- affirmative action programs gone awry. As told here, the failure of these programs has led to an introduction of **terror** into the lives of naval officers. This **campaign of terror** is only the logical result of attempting to social-engineer a fighting organization which is of necessity based on more profound 'natural' truths of 'warriorhood' and the traditional concept of duty, honor, country.

Terror in the U.S. Marine Corps

The above stories are not the only stories of 'terror in the ranks' of the U.S.military. Bill Lind, a former staffer for Senator Robert A. Taft, Jr. (R-OH) and Senator Gary Hart (D-CO) is now the host of the very popular National Empowerment (NET-TV) cable television program, *Modern War*. He is, as well, a military historian of some repute. Lind tells the story of his talk with a group of U.S. Marine Corps officers, young Captains, during which he said (purposely making a chauvinistic joke, in order to observe the

---

148 Argetsinger, Amy, "No 'Systemic Flaw' Found at Naval Academy: Panel Attributes Criminal Behavior by Some Midshipmen to Changes in Outside World," The Washington Post, 31 May 1997.
149 Ibid.
150 Ibid.

reaction)[151], "...*in your post-Cold War world of military 'dominance,' that is 'force dominance' and 'information dominance' over your potential enemies, wouldn't it be nice if you just created a billet for a 'force dominatrix' or 'information dominatrix,' and assign women to these billets. They could have spiffy little uniforms and could excel at this new specialty in the newly feminized Navy.*" Lind said that there was a deathly silence in the room as a result of this heresy. Then someone gushed, "*God, I hope this isn't being tape recorded. We could all be cashiered by listening to this.*"

Lind was astonished. These young Marine officers were **terrified**. They had not said anything offensive at all. But just being caught <u>listening</u> to such speech was enough to send **shivers of terror** through them. Their careers would be at risk. Indeed, the current Navy practice of 'sensitivity training' for enlisted men and officers is a form of **'thought control'** that we have not seen since Stalin's use of such techniques in enforcing 70 years of communist totalitarianism over the population of the former Soviet Union.

<u>Sensitivity Training: a Tool for Neo-Marxist 'Thought Control'</u>

Judge Robert H. Bork reminds us that[152] "*...radical feminism could not be anything but totalitarian in spirit.*" He further reveals that 'thought control' is a major component of this spirit. "*Radical feminism is totalitarian because it denies the individual a private space; every **private thought** and action is public and, therefore, political...the [radical feminist] movement claims the right to **control** every aspect of life...[they wish to] **control our thoughts** as well as behavior.*"

A method used by totalitarian regimes, such as Stalin's Soviet Union, is to invoke 'sensitivity' training. Bork follows this theme in reminding us that[153] "*Multiculturalism, therefore, necessarily requires affirmative action ... Multiculturalism, or diversity, also requires **'sensitivity'** ... Sensitivity, in turn, requires small tyrannies and personal humiliations, or worse. Worse is the destruction of careers and reputations.*" Sensitivity training is a favored tool for feminizing the U.S. Navy.

A senior retired naval officer tells The Author of a 'sensitivity training' session carried out at NAS Patuxent River, MD while he was assigned to the Naval Air Test Center there. These sessions have become common practice throughout the Navy during the 1990s. He was a young Lieutenant at the time (during the early-1970s). A black Chief Petty Officer was giving the training along with a female subordinate who was Hispanic. Surprisingly, the Chief said, "*All of you are racists. [Long pause.] Why? [Another long pause.] Because you are white!*" At this accusation, the young LT rose and protested that he was not a racist, had indeed not participated in anything even remotely related to racist activity or thought, had no known ancestors who owned slaves, and furthermore, had ancestors who fought on the side of the North in the Civil War to emancipate the slaves. The Chief replied, "*Lieutenant, it is clear that you do not have the proper attitude. Your comments are disruptive of this class. You are dismissed.*"

---

151   Lind, Bill, "Modern War: Political Correctness in the Military," NET-TV, 8:00 p.m., 6 December 1996.
152   Ibid, Bork, Robert H., pp. 201.
153   Ibid, Bork, Robert H., pp. 308.

At this, the young LT asked that the Chief step outside for a private conversation. The LT told the Chief that in his Navy a Chief Petty Officer does not 'dismiss' a commissioned officer. In fact, the entire military structure of a 'chain-of-command' would be violated if such a practice were allowed. After some heated words, they decided to let the whole thing drop. The LT left the class. The Chief Petty Officer 'commissar' returned to his class to indoctrinate the remaining naval officers -- the passive sheep, some of whom would become the Navy's flag-rank officers in the 1980s and early 1990s.

This practice of conducting 'sensitivity training' sessions is a common practice in today's military. The move toward multiculturalism and diversity that has taken over our universities and our workplaces has now been thrust upon our military. For example, about 250 senior military and civilian officials met in 1994 for a daylong 'Diversity in Defense' forum[154] sponsored by the Department of Defense. The objective was to "...*focus on numerical goals [quotas] to increase minority representation in the officer ranks.*" William Perry, the Secretary of Defense at the time and under congressional pressure to ensure equal opportunities for women and minorities, "...*recently ordered increased equal opportunity training, especially for senior officers, and commissioned an extensive study of whether discrimination is preventing women and minority officers from reaching senior ranks. He has also re-established the office of deputy assistant secretary for equal opportunity -- a position created in 1963 but abolished in 1986.*" Thus, a great social engineering experiment is being foist on the U.S. military, an experiment of the same magnitude that was foisted on the American people during the 1960s, the welfare state, which has resulted in a near pathological breakdown of American education and urban society. The same result is in store for our nation's military.

The U.S. military is in the throws of a crisis in male-female relations in the wake of the current 'feminization' of our armed forces. It is clear that male-female romantic relations in the military are not 'leadership problems that can be managed.' The recent U.S. Army 'sexual harassment' scandals at the Aberdeen Proving Ground and other training bases is evidence of this crisis. The Clinton administration's program to conduct so-called 'gender sensitivity training' for military personnel is also proof of this failure.

One participant in such training at the Naval Postgraduate School said the following[155]. "*One of our group, a commander who had just completed his tour as commanding officer of a destroyer, raised his concerns about packing young men and women together in close quarters for extended periods at sea. The facilitator's [read feminist indoctrinator] reply: 'Well, commander, it looks like you will have a management problem on your hands.' I am constantly amazed. Debate sex education in schools, and any mention of trying to teach abstinence draws hoots of derision, for the kids can't be expected to control themselves. Talk about rampant sexual activity among a ship's crew and it becomes a 'management problem.' I don't know what happens to the 17-year-olds in high school who can't control themselves that turns them into 18-year-olds who can. We, as a nation need to either 1) decide it is OK to copulate freely when and where the urge strikes (except, perhaps, where food is being served) or 2) admit that the Grand Experiment of integration of the sexes is not necessarily applicable in all cases, and*

---

154 Larson, Ruth, "Pentagon's focus on diversity raises fears about ability to fight," The Washington Times, 25 March 1994.
155 Sapp, Charles N., "Some problems with America's grand experiment," Letters to the Editor, The Washington Times, 2 February 1995.

under all conditions." In the very least, such male-female living arrangements lead to serious fraternization problems which directly degrade morale.[156]

Meanwhile, during 1997, aboard the aircraft carrier USS Nimitz, *"...sailors have been disciplined for holding hands. Yet among the 5,500 men and fewer than 100 women aboard ship, sex has been a problem.*[157] *One couple was recently discovered fornicating inside the huge air-intake ducts of an F-14's [fighter aircraft] engine."* Leadership problem, indeed! Management problem, indeed! Nature rules!

In spite of these obvious problems, the Navy has issued new policy directives, directing that[158] *"pregnancy and parenthood are compatible with a naval career. A woman who is transferred from ship to shore duty because of pregnancy will be returned to the ship or an 'equivalent billet,' after the pregnancy."* Can you imagine a child born to such a female sailor being ripped from its mother's arms a few months after birth while the mother returns to her ship or 'equivalent billet?' Or worse, can you imagine a mother who <u>freely chooses</u> to leave her helpless infant to pursue her naval career? And can you imagine this child being left behind, in many situations, without a mother or a father to care for it? Our 'new' Navy can. This is occurring in today's 'feminized' Navy.

This policy is explained as follows[159]: *"The ban on sex between people serving on ships remains, but shipboard pregnancy will generally not be seen as evidence of wrongdoing, since most sailors have frequent shore leaves. The new policy acknowledges that most pregnant women are able to perform most daily functions well, but may also have special needs."* The U.S. Navy is becoming a free-floating sexual palace with guaranteed U.S. Government support as a substitute for fatherhood! Any active duty naval officer who would stand up against this 'feminization' of the Navy would be summarily

---

[156] Roberts, Paul Craig, "Crying rape to hide failed policy?," The Washington Times, 17 March 1997. 'The Associated Press recently reported that 40 percent of the female Army recruits who brought sexual harassment charges [against Army superiors] now admit they were consensual partners in the sexual activity. In other words, **fraternization** is widespread. Radical feminists, of course, don't admit there is any such thing as consensual sex, and the military brass is so heavily invested in the [Army's] gender integration policy that they, too, prefer to see sexual fraternization as rape. The purpose of military training is to create unit cohesion based on loyalty to comrades. This military ethos is shattered by the introduction of Eros, which replaces cohesion with sexual rivalry. Eros is individual and exclusive in its focus, and gender integration turns comrades into sexual competitors. What is happening is this: Female military personnel suspected of, or caught in, sexual fraternization are given the option of saving their careers and vested benefits by accusing their male partners of rape or harassment. This saves the Army from having to admit that **sexual fraternization** is taking place. When caught, the female can save her career by doing the Army, Navy or Air Force a favor and accusing her male partner of coercion. The Army [is] much more comfortable blaming racism for false accusations than it is in acknowledging that gender integration has loosed Eros in the ranks.'

[157] Barry, John and Thomas, Evan, "Shifting Lines," NEWSWEEK, pp. 36, 16 June 1997.

[158] Scarborough, Rowan, "Navy shifts stance on pregnancy," The Washington Times, 8 February 1995.

[159] Editorial, "Sailing Into Motherhood," The New York Times, 11 February 1995.

dismissed. No hearing. No consideration. No career. The **reign of terror** runs deep in the U.S. Navy.

America No Longer 'Understands' Military Service

Through the 1970s, nearly half the men in America were veterans of military service. Employed throughout business and government, this prior military service ensured an understanding of, if not appreciation for, military service. Since the draft's end in 1972, this number has dropped by half (now 25 percent) and is still falling. This trend indicates that America is retreating from fighting 'democratic' wars, that is, wars participated in by all social and economic classes. Thus, we are returning to a society based on 'class,'[160] just as Great Britain was labelled before World War I.

For example, observe Cokie Roberts (an elite member of America's 'chattering class') berating a young American soldier for having reservations about being sent to Bosnia just weeks before Christmas 1995. On national television, she exclaimed with shock and indignation[161], "*Our military is an all-volunteer force. How can they possibly be hesitant to deploy to Bosnia. They knew the risks when they volunteered.*" Implicit in Ms. Roberts' remark is the idea that '*We pay for your volunteer service. Do your duty.*' Unwittingly, she is actually characterizing an attitude appropriate to a mercenary armed force, willing to do its elite master's bidding because 'we pay for it.'

As another example of America's turning to a 'class-laden' society, Elizabeth Farnsworth[162] , a nationally known interviewer on the MacNeil-Lehrer News Hour, conducted the same conversation (using nearly an identical comment as that of Ms. Roberts) with several tearful and demoralized wives of soldiers about to deploy to Bosnia before Christmas 1995.

In yet another example, Richard Cohen, a nationally syndicated columnist penned[163] "*Such fears [of reprisal if U.S. soldiers capture Bosnian-Serb war crimes indictees] should never be casually dismissed, but really, <u>isn't risk part of being in uniform</u>?*" This Vietnam War dodger is very willing that this 'risk' be shouldered by others in his 'class-laden' society. Indeed, America is harking back to the days when armies were 'non-democratic,' that is, formed on the foundation of privilege and class. Our all-volunteer Army is a throwback to 'pre-democratic' wars. Women are a growing component of this Army. Indeed, America no longer 'understands' military service. Consequently, fewer and fewer Americans understand military service and military power -- its strengths and its limitations.

This situation is true in particular for our current national leadership. President Clinton and his advisors simply do not understand the

---

160 Hynes, Samuel, "The Soldiers' Tale: Bearing Witness to Modern War," pp. 129, The Penguin Press, 1997. Hynes observes that "*The idea that war's tribulations had transformed class-ridden England into a classless society was a powerful part of the special English myth of the war ... In the myth, a democratic war [where everyone served, everyone suffered] had created a truly democratic nation.*"
161 Roberts, Cokie, "This Week with David Brinkley," ABC TV, Channel 7, 11:30 a.m., 3 December 1995.
162 Farnsworth, Elizabeth, "The MacNeil-Lehrer News Hour," PBS, Channel 26, week of 3 December 1995.
163 Cohen, Richard, "Soft on War Criminals," The Washington Post, 9 May 1996.

American military ethos. In fact, they are of a generation that essentially 'loathed' the military. They have become a little more comfortable with the U.S. armed forces when they suddenly realized after the 1992 election that now, *Those troops are ours.*' The implication is that now that they are in power, the use of this power in any way they see fit is somehow all right.

It is ironic that President Clinton and his comrades who opposed the Vietnam War (an elite minority, I might add) and who were instrumental in convincing a majority of the American people that the war was not worth the price in American lives, are now a minority elite who are charging headstrong into military 'peacekeeping' actions against the wishes of the American people. These are the same people who, having treated our armed forces as the enemy during their youth, have been quoted[164] from the viewing stand during the President's inauguration ceremony while Air Force aircraft flew over in formation, "*You know, I used to hate the military. But seeing those planes fly over, I suddenly realized, 'Now, they are mine!' I have changed my mind about the military.*" Indeed, they have. Many of these elite Boomers, who did not play with toy soldiers while children, and 'loathed' the military during their early adulthood, are now in their 40s and early 50s enjoying the game of playing with real soldiers. Only this endeavor is not a game. America's sons have died, their bodies[165] dragged through the streets as people flayed them with sticks and clubs, and had their flesh rendered[166] and delivered in plastic bags to the doorsteps of U.S. agencies in Somalia. Many others will die and be maimed in 'peacekeeping' actions in Bosnia, Albania, Rwanda, and other God-forsaken places -- just as they died and were maimed in Somalia.

Many of the elite and affluent Boomers sat out the Vietnam War in law schools, seminaries, the National Guard, and other combat-deferred alternatives. A combat veteran of that war describes[167] the "*...boys, (mostly teenagers) with whom he served and loved as barely literate, having difficulty telling time, counting money, or reading a map.*" To compound this inequity, much of the Vietnam experience has and is still being defined and shaped by the elite Boomers who successfully eluded service. These people now occupy influential positions in government, education and the media from which they pontificate on our "*moral foreign policy*" and justify their own self-serving[168] actions more than two decades ago.

This dichotomy is brilliantly brought to light in the symbolic gesture of President Clinton's raising the hand of Lewis Puller, Jr. (a former

---

[164] Limbaugh, Rush, "'Excellence in Broadcasting' Radio Talk Show," WMAL-630, remarked daily during the week after the January 1993 inauguration of President William Jefferson Clinton. Limbaugh read from a story in The Washington Post in the weeks after the inauguration. It was attributed (by name) to a mid-1960s hippy who was among the elite who would be 'running the country' for the next eight years.

[165] Yost, Mark, "A Short History of Somalia," The Wall Street Journal, 19 October 1993.

[166] Gertz, Bill, "Retrieving comrades who fell in battle, " The Washington Times, 1 November 1993.

[167] "On Memorial Day: Where was Bill Clinton?" Pamphlet from the Concerned Veterans of America, handed out on Memorial Day during President Clinton's appearance, protested by thousands at the Vietnam Memorial Wall, Memorial Day 1993.

[168] Rosenblatt, Roger, "Coming Apart: A memoir of the Harvard Wars of 1969," 1997.

Marine, confined to a wheelchair, who lost the use of his arms and legs after stepping on a land mine in Vietnam) above their heads as a signal of celebration and healing before the President's 1993 Memorial Day speech at the Vietnam War Monument -- the Wall. Puller, who committed suicide nearly a year later, was disappointed that the President had appointed so few Vietnam War veterans to his administration in his first term. For example[169], fifty percent of male senators ages 39-59 (the Vietnam War/Boomer generation at young adulthood then) were military alumni, as were 50 percent of male representatives and 43 percent of the total male population in that age bracket. Yet only 18 percent of Clinton's Senate-confirmed appointees and 8 percent of senior White House staff in that group are veterans (of any war). (Note: It is estimated [by The Author] that fewer than 10 <u>Vietnam War veterans</u> were appointed[170] to serve in Clinton's first term, out of the approximately 2,000 political positions in the administration.)

It has been publicly reported that[171] *"Lewis Puller told fellow vets that he felt 'used' by Clinton and that the White House was trying to 'co-opt' him."* It is obvious, in the aftermath of Clinton's actions after his performance at the Wall that day that he indeed had 'used' Lewis Puller, Jr. in an attempt to atone for his own obvious shortcomings during the Vietnam War. Indeed, Clinton's obvious hypocrisy was scorned by thousands of Vietnam War veterans[172,173] who protested the President's attendance at the Vietnam War Memorial Wall that day. A Vietnam War veteran who protested that day, observed[174] that while Bill Clinton was "struggling" with his decisions about the war (and protesting against it while visiting Prague and Moscow), *"...a boy in my squad named Randy was shot in the face by an enemy soldier. He struggled to breathe before choking to death on his own blood and bone fragments."*

The President's circumvention of personal sacrifice and risk during the Vietnam War is not indicative of the character traits which have historically personified America's leaders. His blatant exploitation of "the system" to shift the burden of Vietnam service to other less-well-connected youth defies the principles upon which our country was built. For the President, and other elitist Boomers who evaded service during the Cold War (and their enablers in the Silent generation), *'Healing the wounds of Vietnam'* really means *'We want to forget about Vietnam and hide our personal actions during the Cold War.'* The defining experience in the lives of the elitist Boomers, those now in prominent national-level positions, is their evasion of responsibilities during the Cold War. Now, to justify their youthful protests during the 1960s, they are obsessively driven to tear down and destroy the institutions, including the U.S. military, that were so effective in winning the Cold War.

An example of this Boomer-generation obsession with destroying any positive contribution that other Americans may have made in prosecuting the

---

169   Wheeler, John, "Lewis Puller was no stereotypical Vietnam vet: Author-hero symbolized his peers' creative leadership," USA TODAY, 17 May 1994.

170   Broder, David S., "No Veterans Preference in This Administration," The Washington Post, 26 December 1993.

171   Ibid, Wheeler, John, USA TODAY.

172   Brown, Jr., James P., "Mr. President, 'healing' doesn't come on the cheap," Letter to the Editor, The Washington Times, 30 May 1993.

173   Scarborough, Rowan, "Veterans to protest Clinton's Wall talk," The Washington Times, 27 May 1993.

174   Ibid, Pamphlet from the Concerned Veterans of America, Memorial Day 1993.

Cold War is the reporting of the suicide of Lewis Puller, Jr. by the media elite. Eleanor Clift, an elite Boomer and a shrill sycophant of the Clinton administration, writing for Newsweek Magazine[175], '*exposed*' Lewis Puller's account of his tragic loss of limbs to a land mine during combat action in the Vietnam War. Puller's account is presented in his Pulitzer Prize winning autobiography 'Fortunate Son.' Eleanor Clift attempts to diminish the account of the battle action for which Puller won the Silver Star. Interviewing Puller's radioman during that action, she presents a view that diminishes the portrayal of Puller's combat engagement during the time which resulted in his stepping on a land mine. Clift, absolutely devoid of any concept of the 'fog of war' surrounding combat situations, plants the seed of doubt without a shred of evidence in support of her hypothesis. This arrogance, so representative of the elite Boomers who demonstrated against the Vietnam War, is now being foist on the American people in their attempt to completely rewrite the history of our immediate and distant past.

The second term of President Clinton's administration is even less well represented by veterans with military service. Through the 1970s, nearly half the men in America were veterans,[176] employed throughout business and government and ensuring an understanding of, if not appreciation of, military service. Since the draft's end in 1972, this number has dropped by half and is still falling. The number of women professionals, few of whom are veterans, has soared. There are 26 million male veterans and one million female veterans in the United States. Veterans do not hold senior posts in all workplaces, including the Federal Government, in proportion to their share of the population. In the civilian workforce, 37 percent of the men over age 35 are veterans while 51 percent of the men in the Senate and 40 percent of the men in the House of Representatives are veterans. President Clinton sets a national example of barring veterans. Only <u>4 percent</u> of the men on the White House staff are vets and there is not a single woman veteran.[177] Consequently, the nation's domestic and foreign policy is less well formulated when military experience, the common sense, common denominator of what can and what cannot be done militarily, is sparse in our nation's political leadership.

The Mass Media are Even Less Informed of the Military Ethos

The nation's newspapers and television outlets are even less well informed than the Clinton administration or Congress of the military ethos in our American experiment with democracy. Reporters and television producers and anchors are more apt to listen to and repeat the propaganda of those even less well informed than themselves when reporting on military affairs. Consequently, the American people, who are less and less experienced in military affairs, are at the mercy of these ill-informed scribes, television producers, and talk-show hosts for their information and attitudes towards our nation's military.

For example, Bonnie Erbe, the host of the television show, 'To the Contrary,' viewed on PBS, stated[178] "...*there have always been <u>mercenary</u> armies*..." when discussing our all-volunteer force and the impact of women

---

[175] Clift, Eleanor and Adler, Jerry, "Death of a 'Fortunate Son': Lewis Puller Jr.; A hero of survival more than war," NEWSWEEK, pp. 44, 23 May 1994.
[176] Wheeler, John, "Where are our vets?," The Washington Times, 26 February 1997.
[177] Ibid, Wheeler, John.
[178] Erbe, Bonnie, "To the Contrary," PBS-TV, Channel 26, 11:00 a.m., 15 March 1997.

serving in the Army and the enlisted recruits' relatively low socioeconomic status. Obviously, Ms. Erbe has never been exposed to objective history wherein our founding fathers abhorred the idea of a mercenary standing army -- and made provisions against such an army for our nation's future.

Bill Press, a co-host of CNN's 'Crossfire' television program[179], recently asserted that "...*women drove tanks in the Gulf War ...and ... women are 'fighting' now in Bosnia.*" Of course, this is not only uninformed nonsense, it is outright lying on national television. Women were not assigned to combat billets such as tank drivers during the Gulf War. Women do not drive tanks now. And no one is 'fighting' in Bosnia. U.S. troops are essentially performing police functions. A few women are, indeed, billeted as military police, but they are not in combat and they are not 'fighting' anyone. But Bill Press doesn't know the difference and he doesn't care. Not so long as the radical feminist propaganda is spread to the TV viewing audience. And he knows that millions of Americans are not knowledgeable enough to know whether or not he is lying. Nor do they seem to care.

An even more egregious example of lack of knowledge in reporting on military affairs was Evan Thomas, the Washington Bureau Editor for NEWSWEEK magazine, who recently parroted the radical feminist line on women-in-combat (promulgated primarily by lawyers) in both NEWSWEEK[180] and on the CBS-TV political talk show, 'Inside Washington.'[181] He presented the reasons (*the Navy set them up to fail*) that the first five female combat-trained Navy carrier pilots failed on their first deployment aboard the USS Abraham Lincoln and were removed from carrier aviation duty.

The Rebuttal to Evan Thomas' NEWSWEEK Article
The Author rebutted[182], point-by-point, Evan Thomas' description of so-called '*prejudice*' of male naval officers in dealing with the first crop of female 'fighter pilots.' It is fruitful to paraphrase that rebuttal here as an example of the complete lack of understanding by the nation's mass media of what combat naval aviation is and is not.

Mr. Thomas' 17 March Newsweek article, "*Falling Out of the Sky*," is the most one-sided, uninformed gibberish I have yet to see in a major media outlet. He gives himself away when he uses such terms as '*fraternity boys*' and '*clubby world*' to describe carrier naval aviators and their professional environment. That may be a part of his yuppy world but that is not an apt description of the profession of naval aviation.

In addition, it is clear that Mr. Thomas has absolutely no idea of what it takes to be a professional carrier naval aviator. His comment, '*[Nuggets]*[183] *need extra teaching and training to become accomplished at the precarious business of landing jets at sea*," is particularly ill-informed.

---

179 Press, Bill, "Women in Combat," Crossfire, CNN-TV, 7:30 p.m., 3 April 1997.
180 Thomas, Evan and Vistica, Gregory L., "Falling Out of the Sky," NEWSWEEK, pp. 26, 17 March 1997.
181 Thomas, Evan on Gordon Peterson's CBS-TV show (Channel 9), "Inside Washington," 11:00 a.m., 9 March 1997.
182 Atkinson, Gerald L., "Letter to Evan Thomas," 13 March 1997.
183 A 'nugget' is a first-tour carrier naval aviator assigned to an operational squadron which deploys aboard an aircraft carrier. This is his or her first operational combat flying assignment after having completed all primary, advanced, and operational combat training.

Even 'nuggets' are supposed to have demonstrated at least a minimum of aeronautical skills to earn their 'wings of gold.' After all, by the time a pilot reaches a fleet operational squadron, he or she has gone through and presumably mastered the requirements of many stages of flight training. In addition to his or her pre-flight, primary, and advanced flight training (about 16-20 months of intensive flying one-on-one with a flight instructor and other trainees), he or she must progress through familiarization, instruments, tactics and carrier qualification training in the fighter or attack aircraft he or she will fly in the fleet before being assigned to an operational squadron. By this time he or she is not supposed to exhibit substandard flying performance. After all, he or she had supposedly <u>met at least the minimum performance standards</u> at this stage. The epidemic of Field Naval Aviation Evaluation Boards (FNAEBs) (for females and males) in today's Navy is evidence that some of these pilots have not met such standards in their training. This is a stark departure from previous Navy experience. In fact, I had heard of only one FNAEB conducted in any air group in which I served in over 20 years of carrier aviation.

Mr. Thomas' comments that LT Lohrenz was treated with little compassion after her friend LT Kara Hultgreen died in a carrier landing accident shows absolutely no understanding of the psyche of a 'real' combat carrier pilot. For example, he states *"When a pilot is killed, his squadron-mates often take a few days off."* Nonsense! I will never forget the day when I, as a 'nugget,' assigned to a squadron flying the most dangerous fighter in the Navy at the time, the F7U-3M, was on the bridge catwalk with a friend watching daylight landings on the USS Forrestal 'shakedown' cruise. An FJ-3 'Fury,' flown by one of the best aviators in the air wing, made a perfect landing to the three-wire. The arresting cable suddenly snapped and the fighter 'majestically' rose in a slow arc, and flipped over on its back as it crashed into the sea beside the ship. The pilot had no chance. We watched as the aircraft slowly, softly sank from sight -- carrying the executive officer of Fighter Squadron 21 to a watery grave.

My friend and I were astonished, aghast. We simply looked at each other, not speaking, in overpowering awe and disbelief at the spectacle we had just witnessed. Then it hit us at the same time. The pilot had done everything right. And still he died. We flew the <u>next day</u>, bringing one of the world's most under-powered and dangerous jets, the F7U-3M Cutlass, aboard under the guidance of the old 'paddles' landing signal officers.

This was the profession that we had chosen. There was no 'weeping.' There was no hand-holding. There was no commiseration and support in any conversations with either our ship-mates or our superior officers. At such times, each carrier pilot looks deep into his own soul and asks, **'Do I still want to do this**?' I have had over 35 friends, shipmates, and fellow carrier naval aviators die as a result of such 'peacetime' training and wartime tragedies. Anyone in this profession has had the same experience. We did not need any '*adequate support*' as Mr. Thomas decried as being lacking for today's female carrier pilots. We reached down into our own soul for the strength and courage to be a part of a profession that we loved and respected. That is the price we paid. But the benefit we gained was the pure joy of getting out of bed each morning and 'champing at the bit' to meet the day's (or night's) challenge. We loved what we were doing. And we were damn good at it.

A former squadron commander of mine, CAPT Herb Ladley, USN (Retired), is a World War II veteran. He tells of his first carrier qualification in the F4F fighter on the 'paddle-wheel' Wolverine on the Great Lakes. He was a bit high on final approach, decided to go around, and his tailhook caught the top of the barrier (a cable stretched across the deck at a height of about five feet to arrest errant landers). This resulted in the plane slamming down on the deck, becoming partially airborne again and then crashing into the water ahead of the ship. After being fished out of the chilly water, soaked to the skin, he was taken to sick bay, and given a shot of brandy and dry clothing. His squadron commander visited him there and told him to suit up. He was scheduled for a continuation of his carrier qualification that same day. He did. No questions asked. No whining. As any farm boy from the Midwest knows, the best thing to do after being thrown by a horse is to get back on and ride.

Did LT Carey Dunai Lohrenz meet those same standards? In fact, Mr. Thomas' piece completely by-passed the fact that naval aviation training standards at all levels have been gradually reduced over time. This practice, started in the early 1980s and accelerated today, is destroying naval carrier aviation.

Other parts of Mr. Thomas' article are particularly revealing. He stated that LT Lohrenz required "...*10 'passes' at landing on the carrier the day she learned her comrade had died*," and that she told her RIO in the back seat that "*I'm going to have some snakes in the cockpit today.*" My God! Anyone needing ten passes to get aboard ship is a hazard to herself, her back-seater, and her shipmates. These are simply not the flying skills of a qualified carrier aviator. It is no wonder her 'back-seater' had chilly things to say to her. She probably scared the poor guy to death with her 'snake' talk. Those guys in the back seat are utterly and helplessly dependent on their pilot to bring them aboard ship safely. He obviously knew that LT Kara Hultgreen's back-seater had to eject them from her 'out-of-control' jet at the last fraction of a second and he nearly didn't make it. It was her duty to initiate the ejection. She failed in this task. LT Lohrenz, LT Hultgreen's friend, simply didn't understand her responsibility to calm the fears -- maybe even the abject terror -- of her RIO in being assigned to fly with her.

Mr. Thomas' revelation that LT Lohrenz became airsick and '*threw up' later* on during the USS Abraham Lincoln's Persian Gulf cruise is particularly revealing. He also revealed that LT Lohrenz was "...*afraid of a worse fate: coming in too low and cracking up her plane on the fantail.*" Even 'nuggets' are not expected to become airsick. By the time they reach their first operational squadron, they should be well beyond that point, even if they might have become airsick early in their primary flight training. I have never known of a fleet aviator, even a 'nugget,' who became airsick while flying. More importantly, fear has no place in carrier naval aviation. I can honestly say that I have never ever had a 'fear' of hitting the fantail. Neither have any other professional carrier aviators I know. We know it happens. But we do not fear it.

When flying aboard ship, you are so engrossed in the mechanics of flying the aircraft in relation to the ship that you have absolutely no fear. There is no time or place for it. If you are, indeed, fearful of hitting the ramp, your worst fears will eventually be realized. 'Spotting the deck' is one of the cardinal sins in carrier aviation. That is why sound training and operational experience are so important. You are too busy utilizing your professional aviation skills that there is simply no time for contemplation of 'outside' thoughts. Fear of hitting the ramp has no place in the psyche of a carrier naval aviator. If you have such fear, you do not belong. You will die an early death.

Contrary to Mr. Thomas' view, we naval aviators did not and do not use '*drink and carousing*' to '*conquer our fear.*' Fear of everyday dangerous flying tasks has no place in naval aviation. If you have such fear, you are a danger to yourself, your squadron mates, and your ship. You are so busy concentrating on the professional skills honed by a rigorous training and qualification standard that there is simply no place for fear. Contemplation of fear during a dangerous flight is a sure recipe for disaster. A night catapult shot, a night and/or bad weather carrier landing, a flight through a sky that is exploding with bright yellow fireballs and black puffs of anti-aircraft fire do not end favorably if you are guided and/or driven by fear. Only <u>absolute concentration</u> and an <u>uncommon self-control</u> allow you to negotiate those challenges successfully. Those of us who have successfully met those challenges know that rigorous training standards rendered us ready to face adverse circumstances, even when we were 'nuggets.' We used to joke with each other (once we made the final cut) that *'Given enough bananas, you could train a monkey to fly aboard ship.'* Without those rigorous standards, however, all bets are off.

Mr. Thomas sympathizes with LT Lohrenz' comment that women need a large network of 'bonded' females in order to be successful in naval carrier aviation. Nothing could be farther from the truth. One's ability to fly a high performance jet aboard a carrier has absolutely nothing to do with *'bonding or fraternal support.'* It is just between you, your machine, and the carrier deck. You have either mastered the mechanics of this or you have not. Rigorous daily training and absolute concentration render a naval aviator competent. Nothing else matters. It does not depend at all on some ethereal sense of community. You either have mastered the skills required or you have not. If you have not mastered these skills, no amount of *'bonding or fraternal support'* is going to land that aircraft for you, especially in poor weather, at night, and/or with choppy seas.

Another point. Mr. Thomas' comment that *'Landing...a warplane on a heaving deck in the middle of the night is extremely difficult. In the clubby world of naval aviators, macho posturing is a way of fighting off fear, drinking and carousing a way of easing the pressure.'* Carrier aviation is indeed hazardous. That is part of its appeal. But not all carrier aviators are 'macho' posturers and not all *'drink [to excess] and carouse.'* Many of us were quiet, competent, professionals with wives and families who relished the daily challenge of naval aviation. In fact, I have known only a few others who fit the mold of which you speak. But they usually failed. In fact, one such 'macho, drinking, lady-killer,' who constantly bragged of his flying skills during peacetime cruises visited our ship on Yankee Station off the coast of North Vietnam. I asked him, *'Charlie, what in hell are you doing here?'* He said that he was serving as the 'spotting officer' aboard a battleship which was shelling the beach from offshore. His answer. *'I turned in my wings. I just couldn't stand the thought of being shot at.'* Bravado may be the image Mr. Thomas has of naval aviators. But believe me, the good ones, then and now, are those who are relatively quiet, competent, and gentlemanly. But don't get into a fight with them. They are trained to kill.

Mr. Thomas' NEWSWEEK article, typical of the mainstream media, is full of the whining, excuse-making, and silly drivel of a failed cadre of 'would-be' naval aviators. The fact of the matter is that this group of female combat pilots are representative of the failed 'affirmative action' policies that have weakened the Navy over the past sixteen years. The book, "The New Totalitarians: Bosnia as a Mirror of America's Future," details this slide to mediocrity of naval aviation and the U.S. Navy at large. Double standards for females and minorities have, gradually over time, resulted in reduced standards for all. Clear evidence of this decline is revealed in the number of FNAEBs which are being convened in operational combat squadrons.

It is clear that Evan Thomas and others in the media are swallowing the radical feminist propaganda regarding women-in-combat. With the media's ignorance of the military's 'warrior' ethos, how else could it be? The record is clearly showing that this experiment is not working. Training and qualification standards have been lowered. Males as well as females are being 'winged' under reduced standards in naval aviation training. Fighting effectiveness decreases. Morale plummets. We are at increased risk of a catastrophic military failure in the future.

Mr. Thomas' article reveals a direct media bias for the radical feminist position. *"But the experience of the female fliers aboard the Abraham Lincoln...shows that some deep prejudices will have to be overcome before women can be accepted as top guns."* His bias is revealed when he asserts that anyone who is opposed to women-in-combat is prejudiced, and, presumably biased and chauvinistic. In fact, the U.S. Navy experiment with women-in-combat is not working. And those of us who are opposed to women-in-combat, including a vast majority of those who have actually participated in killing other human beings in combat, can stand on evidence, experience, and reason to back our position. It is not *'prejudice.'* It is common sense, backed up by vast experience -- actually over 6,000 years of the latter -- which is at the heart of our opposition to women-in-combat.

'Technology' is no Crutch for Women-in-Combat

Radical feminists often argue[184] that today's high-technology military, that is, combat arms such as naval carrier aviation, does not require physical 'strength.' Consequently, they argue that combat is a working environment in which women can function as 'combat pilots' just as well as men. The nation's mass media have parroted this radical feminist mantra as if it were gospel. This argument has several serious flaws. The major flaw is that it is simply not true.

Physical Differences Between Men and Women

Surprise! Surprise! Men and women are physically different. Differences in anthropometric characteristics and body composition -- size, muscle mass, bone mass, fat distribution, and structure of the elbow joints and pelvis -- favor men over women in strength, explosive power, speed, and throwing and jumping. Cardiorespiratory differences -- size of heart and lungs, oxygen content, oxygen uptake (volume of oxygen that can be extracted from inspired air), average hemoglobin content, body temperature, and sweat gland function -- give men an advantage in physical endurance and heat tolerance.[185]

As an example of how these disadvantages affect women in the armed forces, studies involving Army recruits, indicate women are at a higher risk

---

184 For example, see Lohrenz, Carey, LT USN, "Women in the Military," MSNBC-TV '@ Issue,' Host Edie Magnus with guests COL Kelly Hamilton, USAF (Retired), LT Carey Lohrenz, LtCol Rhonda Cornum, U.S. Army, and Dr. Gerald L. Atkinson, CDR USN (Retired), 3:00 p.m., 18 March 1997. LT Lohrenz, asserted on national television that the first crop of female Navy 'fighter pilots' all failed in their first deployment on the USS Abraham Lincoln because, *"They did not have a network of women to talk to and were given the 'silent treatment' by the male aviators."* She further asserted that females are as capable of males in Navy combat aviation because *"...technology is rendering 'strength' obsolete in combat aviation."*

185 Binkin, Martin, "Who Will Fight the Next War?: The Changing Face of the American Military," pp. 31, The Brookings Institution, 1993.

for exercise-induced injuries than men. Compared to men, women had 2.13 times greater risk for lower extremity injuries and a 4.71 times greater risk for stress fractures. The men sustained 99 days of limited duty due to injury while women incurred 481 days of limited duty[186].

The Presidential Commission on the Assignment of Women in the Armed Forces heard testimony that[187], "...*women, in general, are shorter, weigh less, have less muscle mass and have a greater relative fat content than men. In terms of military significance, women are at a distinct disadvantage when performing military tasks requiring a high level of muscular strength and aerobic capacity, due to their lower muscle mass and greater relative fat mass. The dynamic upper torso muscular strength of women is approximately 50 to 60 percent that of men, while their aerobic capacity is approximately 70 to 75 percent that of men.*"

Women's aerobic capacity is significantly lower than that of men, meaning they cannot carry as much as far as men can, and they are more susceptible to fatigue. In terms of physical capability, the <u>upper five percent</u> of women are at the level of the <u>male median</u>. This means that in the very physically demanding ground combat environment, as a unit extends the physical envelope of its members, the men have room to improve, whereas the women have already reached the upper end of their limits. The average <u>20-to-30 year-old woman</u> has the same aerobic capacity as a **50 year-old man**. Armed forces <u>cannot win wars with 50-year olds</u>.

Strength, Stamina, and Endurance are Required in Combat Aviation

A friend of The Author was blown out of the sky over Laos during the Vietnam War. He ejected from his flaming jet and landed in a dense underbrush beneath a growth of very tall trees. He hid in the thick undergrowth. The enemy was quickly nearby, searching the thick brush for him. Beating the bushes. Shouting to each other. Shooting. The next day, after a night of evasion, he called in the helicopter rescue team on his hand-held radio. In time, the UH-34D rescue helicopter hovered overhead and lowered its long 150 foot 'rescue cable' into the pilot's vicinity. The Pilot was in radio contact, directing the helicopter to his position. Just when the rescue 'horse collar,' on the end of a steel cable, was within a short distance of the downed pilot's position, he jumped up from his hiding position in the bushes on the side of a hill and ran to grab it. He[188] "...*sprinted down the hill and leaped as high as he could. He thrust his right arm through the collar but could not get his left arm into it. In desperation he locked his left hand over his right wrist and hung on with **all his strength**.*" Just then the enemy started shooting at the helicopter. The downed pilot hung on to the collar for dear life. As the helicopter beat a hasty retreat, the enemy filled the sky with automatic weapons fire as the pilot, with <u>only his upper body strength</u>, maintained his precarious hold on the collar.

The helicopter with its dangling human load climbed to 500 feet, then 1,000 feet, 1,500 feet and finally 2,000 feet while both the pilot and the helicopter were being shot at from below. Automatic AK-47 weapons fire was

---

186 The Presidential Commission on the Assignment of Women in the Armed Forces, "Women in Combat: Report to the President," pp. 9, Brassey's, 1993.
187 Ibid, pp. 13.
188 Wilson, George C., "Flying the Edge: The Making of Navy Test Pilots," Naval Institute Press, pp. 1-13, 1992.

zinging past both the pilot, hanging on the collar for his life, and the helicopter. The rescue crew did not have the time to wind the rope upward into the helicopter to pull the pilot to safety, as is the normal procedure. If the pilot's <u>upper body strength</u> had failed him, he would have fallen hundreds of feet to a certain death. He <u>held on with one arm</u> and was rescued.

Female naval aviators have passed through a military training system wherein the physical standards, including upper body strength, have been substantially reduced ever since they entered the U.S. Naval Academy and other officer training programs in 1976. As a group, women do not have the same physical endurance, stamina, and strength as their male counterparts. Indeed, **physical strength** is still a requisite for survival in naval aviation combat.

Another example. A shipmate of The Author, LT Dieter Dengler, was shot down in Laos while flying his A-1H Skyraider from the deck of the USS Ranger in 1966. He was imprisoned[189] in a jungle Pathet Lao prison camp, Hoi Het, for five months. There he lived on rotten rice and thin gruel. He and six others escaped and fled into the jungle. He and another American, a U.S. Air Force pilot, paired up and wandered through almost impenetrable terrain with little to live on but the rice they carried in bamboo tubes, snakes, iguana and water they drank from streams. During the 23 days that he wandered around trying to 'walk to the ocean' and 'back home to the Ranger,' they both picked up malaria, worms, fungus, and other infections that took a terrible toll on their strength, endurance, and stamina.

But one event, related to the importance of these physical qualities in 'combat' situations, is as follows. While stealthily making their way through tangled underbrush, outlying trails used by Laotian villagers, and mountain streams, Dieter and his friend became very weak, desperate, and drained of stamina. Dieter had to half-carry, half-drag his sick friend through the brush, over karst[190] ridges, and along cold streams. <u>Male strength</u>, stamina, and endurance were the major attributes in his and his friend's ability to survive.

Finally, one day as they rounded a bend in a trail, they stumbled upon a child and his dog. Immediately thereafter a villager appeared, waving a machete over his head. Dieter and his friend knelt, too weak to run, cupped their hands in prayer, and begged the villager to do them no harm. Heedless, the villager hacked Dieter's friend in the groin with a fierce blow. The second swing severed his head from his body, blood spurting in bursts all over the participants. As Dieter moved his hands forward to protect himself from a mortal blow from the machete, the villager suddenly turned and ran -- fearing what he perceived as an offensive maneuver by the *Americali*. Dieter ran and evaded his pursuers in the jungle. Later that night, maddened by what he had witnessed and hallucinating from severe malnutrition, Dengler went back to a thatch village and burned it to the ground.

Twenty-three (23) days after his escape, Dengler was miraculously rescued by a chance sighting of him by a lone Skyraider pilot flying a 'familiarization' flight up the ravine in which Dieter had spread himself on

---

189 Dengler, Dieter, "Escape from Laos," Presidio, 1979.
190 Karst is a hard, crumbly grey rocky material which forms vast sharp cliffs and perilous craggy ridges. These karst landscapes rise out of the heavily forested Laos countryside.

a rock to die. After his six-month ordeal, Dengler weighed only 90 pounds -- 70 pounds down from his normal 160 pounds. He was so weak that he had to be carried to the bathroom. Indeed, strength, stamina, and endurance are prime requisites for combat pilots. Their combat survival depends on it.

Proponents of women-in-combat agree that strength, stamina, and endurance may be factors that render women unable to perform infantry combat duties but deny that women cannot perform combat aviation and combat shipboard duties as well as duties in artillery and armored vehicles. This flies in the face of past U.S. experience in warfare. An Air Force medal of Honor recipient and Vietnam POW, Lance Sijan, found[191] "*In the short time it took him [Sijan] to parachute to earth, he would travel from the relative security of the twentieth century's most advanced military technology to a jungle where the rules and conduct of combat had not undergone any major alteration since Neolithic times.*" Indeed, Dieter Dengler's escape-and-evasion story is a telling reminder of this truth.

Louis Morton, who wrote the official Army history of the Philippines campaign in The Fall of the Philippines, described a situation wherein the Japanese destroyed two-thirds of the American planes in the Philippines on December 8, 1941. This forced fighter pilots and ground crews to fight as <u>combat infantry</u> during the fall of Bataan and Corregidor.

Evidence mounts for high physical strength even during the Gulf War. If assigned to combat positions on an equal basis, women aviators would have had the responsibility to rotate into Air Liaison Officer (ALO) positions with Army ground combat units. According to Air Force Captain Ron Gaulton, who flew A-10s in the Gulf War[192], "*When Desert Storm kicked off, [some pilots] were immediately sent down to the 24th Infantry Division...and were shipped over, and they spent the entire Shield/Storm <u>on the ground</u> with the <u>forward forces</u>, and those were the guys that actually directed the A-10 strikes in [to the target]...So they lived out of the Army, they're right <u>on the front lines</u>, and they are...for all intents and purposes...<u>Army people</u>.*"

An Air Force fighter pilot has testified that[193] "*..The physical demands encompassed in this area are tremendous. The high speeds of the modern aircraft...the high rates of turn that require the high instantaneous G-loads that literally makes your body shake or may put you in G lock..the current requirement for sustaining consciousness is strength and endurance, and to us that is overall stamina.*"

Modern fighter aircraft have control surfaces which are completely driven by hydraulic and electrical systems. The 'stick,' with which the pilot controls the aircraft's flight, is artificially given spring-driven forces so that the pilot doesn't inadvertently over-control and overstress the aircraft with large, rapid stick movements. In fact, stick-force-per-g is a design factor that purposely imposes a muscular force by the pilot on the stick so that the aircraft cannot be damaged by pilot input. These stick forces are fairly light for normal flying but in combat they can be quite high -- up to several tens-of-pounds per g. This force doesn't require extraordinary pilot strength but in a combat dog fight, under very high-g loads (both positive and negative) and vigorous stick-maneuvering by the pilot, high stamina is a very important requirement. For those with low arm-strength, this force, required over a relatively long period of time,

---

[191] The Presidential Commission on the Assignment of Women in the Armed Forces, "Women in Combat: Report to the President," pp. 69, Brassey's, 1993.
[192] Ibid, pp. 69.
[193] Ibid, pp. 67.

drains one's stamina. Consequently, those with relatively low stamina (females in particular) are disadvantaged in combat maneuvering against a determined enemy.

Females are disadvantaged in both strength and stamina in flying fighter aircraft in combat. An experienced FRS flight instructor told The Author that the first few females who were trained in fighter aircraft in the East Coast FRS had to be sent off-base to special weight-lifting and strength training in order to meet the physical rigors of air-combat maneuver training. They simply did not have the strength or stamina to accomplish prolonged combat maneuvers without this extra special physical training.

Jerry R. Cadick, a retired Marine fighter pilot, who has seen war first-hand, tells us that[194] "...*Anybody who says technology levels the playing field, and gender matters not, has never been in sustained, life-threatening combat. Technology matters not a whit. The human response that gripped our ancestors' stomachs and made them want to vomit when they crossed stone axes was, I betcha, identical to mine diving into the hell called North Vietnam ... Fighter pilots, above all else, know who among their peers are 'hunters' and who are the 'hunted.' They absolutely will **not** fly into a known tough combat situation with a wingman they don't trust, and not all men make the cut. Something akin to bonding has to occur in this ancient ritual called war. The few female Naval Aviators are complaining about being on the outside looking in. The media are starting to tar and feather the Navy for lack of zeal in the stampede toward correctness. Where we work is a vicious place ... You're in a machine that is so fast and powerful that you instinctively know that if death comes, it will be full of hot fire ... you will be shred into bits and pieces. Worst of all, you'll be alone in a fierce place where your comrades cannot hold on to you while you die ... We buried one out of four who tried to make a 20-year career ...*" So much for the female Navy 'combat pilots' (e.g. LT Carey Lohrenz) who long for a 'network' of women with whom to commiserate. 'Real' Navy Jet Fighter Pilots get used to it. When pilots die in combat aviation, they will most likely die alone -- engulfed in flames and in 'bits and pieces.'

In a comment delineating the difference between peacetime training and actual war, Cadick observes "...*Citizens, or [Congress] believe that women can be Fighter Pilots ... Politicians weave tales wherein physical differences, being moot in the cockpit, make that an ideal place for a woman. They say that if she can complete the training, then ... she is qualified. In 26 years in the USMC, some of the most skilled officers in the five units I commanded were women. I knew some female Naval Aviators and they were pilots as good as can be found in the nose of any American passenger airliner. If we talk about flying (the art of) from point A to Point B, then many humans qualify handily ... But we ain't talking flying here. We gotta get down to basics, like where we evolved from and some real hard natural selection rules ...*"

Cadick goes on to observe about women-in-combat, "*Guess what, you are bumping up against millions of years of genetic conditioning. Good F---ing Luck! The only test of who can function in combat is combat. In war, first order of business, throw damn near all peacetime training rules overboard. All combat veterans know of plenty of situations where someone was eased into a noncombat function on account of not having what it takes.*

---

[194] Cadick, Jerry R., "On Being a Warrior: Anyone who says technology levels the playing field hasn't been in sustained combat," NEWSWEEK, pp. 16, 14 April 1997.

What it takes wasn't written anywhere, but we knew." This veteran 'warrior,' tested by the trauma of real war, has it right.

Combat aviation is not the only situation where strength, stamina, and endurance are important. The same physical requirements are obvious to anyone who has served aboard a combatant naval vessel. A recent documentary[195], "Aircraft Carrier," revealed the endurance required of sailors operating around the clock while deployed, often with only four to six hours sleep. If a sailor with a critical job is not attentive, it could result in death, his own or that of a pilot or other crew-member dependent upon his performance of duty.

For example, from October 1994 through February 1995, the Commander of the Pacific Fleet ordered two special stand-downs due to a rash of Navy Jet crashes[196] -- involving seven aircraft and four deaths in four months (one was the death of the first female fighter pilot during routine carrier landing practice). During a stand-down, all flying was cancelled (in this case for all Pacific Fleet squadrons) and pilots and maintenance crews attended meetings on safety. It is not clear whether or not gender issues played a part in this rash of accidents. The U.S. Navy leadership had nary a clue as to its apparent 'safety' problem. Navy leaders would only comment that *"Naval aviators are not out of control."* This statement reveals that the Navy leadership either does not know that their 'feminization' and 'affirmative action' policies are destroying their Navy or they know this truth but will not speak up for fear of ending their careers.

In addition, crew members of naval vessels face hazards other than direct combat. According to Samuel Eliot Morison's History of U.S. Naval Operations[197] in World War II, *"On 1 July 30, 1945, a Japanese submarine sank the heavy cruiser USS Indianapolis. Of 1,199 crewmen, roughly 800 successfully abandoned ship. Only 316 survived three-and-a-half days in the water. The others died of exposure or were killed by sharks."* Survival at sea required at least a minimum standard of swimming and/or floating proficiency. Stamina and endurance are the physical attributes that saved the survivors.

One does not have to be reminded of myriad studies comparing strength, stamina and endurance of men versus that of women to know that women are disadvantaged in these measures. Anyone who has grown up in a mixed-gender environment knows this common-sense revelation by practical experience. Only in the elite non-serving elements of America would we expect this to be even the subject of serious discussion. The fact that these are primary requirements of a military combatant, wherever deployed; in infantry, armor, artillery, air, or ship is also universally known to those who have experienced combat.

In 1976, General William C. Westmoreland, former Army chief of staff said[198] *"Maybe you could find one woman in 10,000 who could lead in combat, but she would be a freak and we're not running the military academy for freaks...The pendulum has gone too far...They're asking women to do impossible things. I don't believe women can carry a pack, live in a*

---

[195] NOVA, "Aircraft Carrier," PBS TV, Channel 26, 8:00 p.m., 19 April 1994.
[196] Crawley, James W., "Navy air chief in Pacific tours with safety worries," The Washington Times, 5 February 1995.
[197] The Presidential Commission on the Assignment of Women in the Armed Forces, "Women in Combat: Report to the President," pp. 75, Brassey's, 1993.
[198] Ibid, Binkin, pp. 33.

foxhole or go a week without taking a bath." He was backed up by retired Brigadier General Elizabeth P. Hoisington, a former director of the Women's Army Corps, *"In my whole lifetime I have never known ten women whom I thought could endure three months under actual combat conditions."* These opinions are born out by the record of modern combat.

LTG Binford Peay, U.S. Army, has testified to the Presidential Commission on Women in Combat that[199] *"In fact, technology has made today's battlefield a more lethal, violent, shocking and horrific place than it has ever been. Paradoxically, the last war may have, to external audiences and the uninitiated, appeared clean and very easy. We need only to contemplate for a single moment man's inhumanity to his fellow man and the irrational nature of ethnic conflicts today to get an appreciation that the face of battle has not changed. It is just that we recently have not been involved in the horror as it passes before us on the nightly news..."* Other 'warriors' with more direct and recent hand-to-hand combat experience support this view.

Sgt Maj Harold Overstreet, USMC told the Commission what ground combat involves on a personal level: *"We say 'Combat is combat is combat.' I'm here to tell you, it is not. First of all, I'm here to tell you that it is one thing to be in a combat area; it's another thing to be in a combat area and to have rounds coming in on you. It's even another thing to send rounds down range. But it's a little bit different when you know that you are the guy that is going to have to seek out, close with, and do whatever it takes to kill the enemy. You. You're going to go out there and confront him, one on one. You realize that this is no game, there is no second place, and if you are second place, you don't come back."* He might as well have added that *"...this is also not just a career -- a job a with bureaucratic job description."*

Sgt Maj Overstreet went on to describe what he had experienced in Vietnam[200]. *"...this is two Marine companies that has run into a North Vietnamese regiment. No sooner than they had made contact than six NVA soldiers come dashing right through the lines, and where did they come dashing through to? To the young company commander by the name of Captain Stackpole, and his radio operator. They ended up in the same fighting hole as he did. Well, when six NVA soldiers show up in your fighting position, there is not a lot of time to negotiate. So, immediately, Captain Stackpole pulled his .45 and shot the first two coming into his position. They fell in the hole. About the time they fell in the hole, there's four other individuals in the hole with him and his radio operator. While they're thrashing around in the mud and the blood and the fog of battle, Captain Stackpole loses his pistol. Now, what does he do? With arms and legs and AK-47s thrashing around all over the area, he pulls his K-bar knife, the only thing that he could find at the time. He pulls his K-bar and finally gets a hold of one of the NVA, sticks him in the groin, and rips him all the way to his appetite. While thrashing around, he grabs a hold of the third one, cuts his throat. At the same time, the radio operator cleaves the next one in the head with an E-tool, and Captain Stackpole then stabbed the sixth one to death in the fighting hole. Now, that does take a little bit of upper body strength; it does take a little bit of aggressiveness, as you can obviously see."*

---

[199] The Presidential Commission on the Assignment of Women in the Armed Forces, "Women in Combat: Report to the President," pp. 62, Brassey's, 1993.
[200] Ibid, pp. 63.

Radical feminists today point to the 'fact' that warfare is becoming more of a computerized push-button endeavor where the physical strength and stamina, as described above, is not a factor. The surprisingly short duration of the Gulf Storm War enforced this 'virtual reality' version of the nature of future warfare. This rationale has been presented to support the entry of women pilots in combat aircraft units. This rationale is not and has never been supported by the facts.

Oftentimes, the demarcation is subtle between the true 'warrior' and those who just go through the motions for career-enhancement. In Vietnam, one could distinguish the true 'warrior' aviators from the 'ticket-punching careerists' by observing who carried ball ammunition for their pistols. In peacetime, military pilots were allowed only tracer ammunition for their pistols. Such ammunition was helpful in signalling distress if downed at night or in hazardous terrain and aided in rescue attempts. During the Vietnam War, pilots were given the option[201] of carrying either ball ammunition (for killing people) or tracer ammunition. Tracer ammunition is useless for killing people. The true 'warriors' chose to carry ball ammunition, signaling their inclination to carry the fight to the enemy on the ground if shot down and/or killing captors who might attempt to foil a helicopter evacuation.

The 'ticket-punching careerists' invariably chose tracer ammunition. So, even in those combat roles which do not primarily involve close hand-to-hand with the enemy, it is not unusual that personnel in these roles will find themselves in a hand-to-hand combat situation with the enemy. We must prepare all combatants in our armed forces for such an eventuality. Females will be as disadvantaged in this environment as they would be in infantry hand-to-hand combat situations. Women are simply not physically equipped to fight against men and 'win' as Captain Stackpole fought in his foxhole. Future combat will be no different in this regard than in the past. Strength, stamina, and endurance will be the deciding factors.

The Presidential Commission provided expert combat-veteran testimony, such as that presented above, concerning the pre-eminence of strength, stamina, and endurance in combat. Unfortunately, this testimony was not placed in a prominent position in the report. In addition, Congress and the Clinton administration completely disregarded the commission's cautionary report while authorizing women to participate in combat roles in aviation and aboard some combatant ships. The Pentagon's special Defense Advisory Committee on Women in the Services (DACOWITS) advised against[202] allowing women to serve in field artillery, special operations aviation fields, and a string of other near-combat positions in forward-deployed headquarters. Nevertheless, Army Secretary Togo West proposed opening such positions to women.

After extensive research, Canada has found little evidence to support the integration of women into ground combat units. Of 103 Canadian women who volunteered to join infantry units, only one graduated from the initial training course[203]. Closer to home, U.S. Marine Corps Staff Sergeant Barry

---

[201] Atkinson, Gerald L., Personal Experience as a Combat Naval Aviator on the USS Ranger on Yankee Station during the Vietnam War, December 1965-September, 1966, The Author of this book.

[202] Scarborough, Rowan, "Advisory board never OK'd plan for women in combat," The Washington Times, 30 September 1994.

[203] The Presidential Commission on the Assignment of Women in the Armed Forces, "Women in Combat: Report to the President," pp. 64, Brassey's, 1993.

Bell, who served as a combat engineer during Operation Desert Storm, illustrated these points in his testimony before the Commission. "*My rucksack when I went in weighed 75 pounds. And I walked 12 miles from the border to the mine field. If you're not in peak physical condition during this type of environment, you're not going to be able to perform. And, unfortunately, we weren't in peak physical condition...it kicked our butts...we were bent over, our backs were killing us. The weight was just way too heavy for us, let alone a female Marine or female soldier...Physically, they are just unable to do it. If we were almost unable to do it, I know we would have a hard time pulling the female Marines up to where we were at. Physically, they are just not capable of performing everything we are able to do...*"

Army LTC Douglas Tystad, an M-1 tank commander, told the Commission: "*My view is that the physiological requirements, the strength requirements, are extreme. The stress over time, stamina is required. In my experience, limited though it may be, I've met very few women that I believe could handle the stress, coupled with the physical requirements that we have. At this level, you are down at what the military psychologists and sociologists call the primary group. A crew is a primary group, and we believe that in combat motivation you fight for the primary group. And the group is only as good as its weakest member...*"

For the issue of women-in-combat, we disregard the voice of these expert witnesses at our peril. If we persist, we will have an armed force that either will not fight or cannot fight. Our national security depends on us to make wise choices in this area or we will perish.

The Move Away from Technology Education at the U.S. Naval Academy

The 'high-technology' argument is doubly wrong for women in combat naval aviation. If 'technology' is, indeed, the wave of the Navy's future, the service must recruit from those who have aptitude for, and train and educate its naval officers in the fundamentals of mathematics, science, and engineering. Unfortunately, the trend is away from such disciplines. As more women and minorities matriculate at the U.S. Naval Academy, more and more midshipmen choose a Liberal Arts curriculum laced with History, Political Science, and other non-technical subjects. In fact, one former USNA professor[204] tells of the scholarly rallying cry of today's naval midshipmen, "*Poly-Sci, QPR high!*" This indicates the current trend at the academy to bolster the midshipmens' quality point rating, i.e. their course grades, by taking easier, less challenging courses. This trend, in which the Political Science Department (headed by a female naval officer) is the largest one at the academy, is ominous for a service that is relying more-and-more on 'high technology.' Females at the Naval Academy predominantly take liberal arts courses. This directly refutes the radical feminist argument that females have a place in combat arms which are becoming more-and-more 'technology' dependent; making unnecessary the requirements of strength, stamina, and endurance.

Of course, the outstanding midshipmen still attend the Naval Academy in as many numbers as in previous decades but the middle-to-lower group of

---

204 Anonymous, "Private Conversation," 3 May 1996. This source taught engineering courses for many years at the Naval Academy at Annapolis. He must remain anonymous as a protection against retaliation against his career since he still has young children to put through college. Exposure would bring an end to his professional career.

academically-challenged midshipmen are dragging the academic standards down in all of the technology classes. COL Kelly Hamilton's recent public assertion that[205] "...*the reason so many 'pass' [flight training] is the caliber of people going through is very high. We don't take a lot of people into the military anymore. And we are very particular about those who do come through. Therefore, we are apt to pick and choose and the caliber of people is extremely high [compared to years past].*" This assertion is belied by the facts. Even at the Navy's premiere officer training program, the U.S. Naval Academy, the remedial nature of the academic instruction is of such substandard quality that remediation, subtly but surely, has reduced the standards of quality instruction in all engineering classes. The USNA professors had to teach to the level of the substandard midshipmen rather than to higher levels as in years past.

The USNA professors, described above, confirmed The Author's findings regarding the adverse effects of adjusting standards to achieve social goals in naval aviation with their own experience at the the U.S. Naval Academy. They confirmed that the same process is well entrenched at the Naval Academy and that it is no longer possible for a faculty member to set standards independent of outcomes. Their view of the situation is as follows:[206]

"*Standards are set based on desired political outcomes rather than on the inherent merit of the standard. If a standard does not produce the desired outcome, it is deemed inappropriate regardless of its merit; if a standard produces the desired outcome it is not questioned, regardless of its lack of merit. This lowering of academic standards to meet political goals is directly related to the political pressures over the past fifteen or more years to meet social engineering goals. Most admitted to the Academy are outstanding individuals, but an increasingly significant number of those admitted fail to meet the academic standards of the past. In recent years, the Academy has added a Counseling Center, remedial courses, outside contracting for teaching remedial reading and writing, and a new track to allow those who require such remedial studies to count their remedial courses toward the graduation requirement in place of the high-end courses that midshipmen in the 'traditional' track must take. Courses that have been identified as too challenging have been eliminated or 'redesigned to be more reasonable to the needs of today's midshipmen.' Mental challenges are disparaged by administrators as being of no educational value because, it is argued, the answers to those challenges are not facts a naval officer is ever likely to need to know, and 'unreasonable' mental challenges contribute to preventing certain groups from entering the hard sciences and engineering. Many courses, especially those in math, engineering, and science, have had their syllabi adjusted to allow more and more time for remedial work. This is driven by the need to pass as many as possible, which they identify as a philosophy driven by an underlying goal for diversity at the expense of excellence. The most capable, regardless of their physical features (race, gender, etc.) are no longer allowed the same level of mental challenge as once was acceptable at the Academy for 'the best and the brightest,' because those standards conflict with the necessary political outcomes.*"

The fact-of lowered engineering education standards over time has shown up in unexpected places. It appears that the Naval Academy has not educated enough graduates in the engineering disciplines to replace uniformed

---

205 Ibid, COL Kelly Hamilton, USAF (Retired) on MSNBC-TV show '@ Issue,'
206 Anonymous professors at the U.S. Naval Academy, "Private communication," 6 June 1996.

instructors in these disciplines. A recent notice[207] in NAVY TIMES reveals that "*The Naval Academy is looking for up to 15 <u>Naval Reserve officers</u> to serve as instructors for the 1997-98 school year...The academy is experiencing shortfalls of qualified instructors in the science, mathematics, and engineering departments...Instructors with a master's degree or higher are needed in the areas of computer science, chemistry, mathematics, physics, aeronautical engineering, electrical engineering, mechanical engineering, control systems engineering, naval systems engineering...*" Evidently, the Navy's 'dumbing down' of its standard science and engineering curriculum over time has led to a paucity of qualified regular officers to fill the ranks of instructors in these disciplines.

There is documentary proof of lowered academic standards in high-technology disciplines at the Naval Academy. In 1990, as mentioned before, a civilian chairman of the electrical engineering department was relieved of his post in mid-semester because he refused to raise preliminary grades across the board in two electrical engineering courses and refused[208] to raise grading curves 'across the entire [electrical engineering curriculum].' Midshipmen had complained that "...*they are being given too hard a time.*" Many midshipmen were choosing humanities rather than the academy's traditional high-technology majors.

The chairman of the Electrical Engineering Department was removed because[209] "...*he refused a directive [from the military authority] to arbitrarily raise grades given by other instructors in three required courses in electrical engineering.*" The military leaders had been concerned that midshipmen were receiving low grades in electrical engineering for some time. As revealed earlier in this book, "*For the fall 1989 semester, more than 40 percent of midshipmen in three introductory engineering courses received Ds or Fs.*" Clearly, the midshipmen did not live up to the exacting standards of math, science, and engineering as had their predecessors of years past. This trend has moved the Navy's premiere officer training program away from high-quality technology -- that is, engineering -- education. Such a trend starkly contradicts in practice the radical feminist mantra that 'technology' renders the cockpit 'female friendly.' Very few females at the U.S. Naval Academy take courses rich in engineering disciplines. The standards have been lowered. This reduction of standards has been carried right through to naval carrier aviation.

COL Hamilton's assertion of '...[the military has the] highest caliber of people of all time..." is, therefore, wrong for the U.S. Naval Academy. It is also wrong for naval aviation. The U.S. Navy has recently revealed that women and minorities are 'washed out', that is, attrited from 'strike' jet aviation training, at a rate <u>four times</u> that of white males. Even those who see the disparity as evidence of **bias** <u>against women and minorities defend</u> the Navy's advanced jet training program. For example, they say that[210] "*Women and minorities entering the program are <u>not of the highest caliber,</u> unlike the white men in the program, because corporate competition*

---

207 Short takes, "Academy seeks instructors," NAVY TIMES, 21 April 1997.
208 Weil, Martin and Leff, Lisa, "Naval Academy Relieves Head of Department: Chairman Was Asked to Raise Grades," The Washington Post, 25 February 1990.
209 Mitchell, Brian, "Firing raises old questions about academy's role: Institution again debates 'university' idea at Annapolis," NAVY TIMES, 19 March 1990.
210 Heines, Vivienne, "A Striking Difference: Is Navy combat jet training fair to women and blacks?," pp. 12, NAVY TIMES, 10 March 1997.

woos the best minority and female candidates into better-paying civilian jobs." The fact is that the Navy's 'affirmative action' policy in naval aviation training has reduced the <u>minimum</u> standards for all.

The Absence of Military Standards in Navy Boot Camp

Every tough old Navy enlisted salt has stories to prove their merit. As recruits, they endured a baptism of fire at the Navy's boot camps. Deprived of sleep and lonely for home, they were introduced to military life by somebody barking orders. They marched everywhere, endlessly. *"Fear and intimidation,"* said CAPT Cornelia de Groot Whitehead, the first woman[211] to serve as the commander of the Great Lakes Naval Training Center, now the Navy's only boot camp. *"That was the tradition."*

Times have changed. The Navy now has training divisions that mix men and women together in roughly equal numbers. Boot camp leaders tell new recruits about their <u>rights</u>, and encourage them to <u>file grievances</u> if faced with 'abusive' behavior. As an article in NAVY TIMES recently put it, *"This is not your father's Navy."*

On the night they arrive at boot camp, recruits now get a decent night's sleep. They are even given a little blue card, with lists of places to turn for help, like a chaplain. *"In the dumps?"* the card reads. *"Thinking about running away? Help is less painful!"* It adds, *"Remember, we do **care** about you!"*

CAPT Whitehead who boasts three degrees, including a doctorate in education, has never done a sea tour of duty.[212] Neither has her Executive Officer, CDR Xzana Tellis, who has a master's degree in education. These in-house Navy feminists have overhauled the boot camp curriculum over the past two years so that 'old salts' would not recognize it.

A recent NAVY TIMES article[213] trumpets *"This is not your father's boot camp."* It announces that *"...This really, truly is a kinder, gentler boot camp, reformed for a new generation of recruits who might not be as tough -- or as well grounded in basic values -- as recruits of yesteryear."* In fact, recruit training today bears so little resemblance to what thousands of bluejackets remember of their grinding days in boot camp that some might simply be astounded. *"Recruits no longer drill with rifles and no longer salute their seniors in the enlisted ranks ... the changes are rooted in a premise ... Boot camp should prepare recruits for the 'real Navy' [where no one salutes senior enlisted petty officers and no one carries a rifle]."*

This 'go-easy' approach brings howls from many in the Navy who have been confronted by sailors demanding to know why they're being given an order, especially if they don't really want to follow it. Several visiting chief petty officers worry that boot camp might be getting a little too soft,[214] that the new approach to recruit training already is sending to the fleet sailors who aren't prepared for the discipline demanded of military life. *"If they don't know how to follow,"* said one, *"they won't learn how to lead."*

---

211   Johnson, Dirk, "New Messages Sent At Navy Boot Camp: A Focus on Treating All Recruits Better," The New York Times, 17 March 1997.
212   "Who's running the show," NAVY TIMES, pp. 14, 28 October 1996.
213   Burlage, John, "This is not your father's boot camp: Has Great Lakes gone too soft on recruits?," NAVY TIMES, pp. 12, 28 October 1996.
214   Ibid, pp. 13.

It's still pitch-dark outside when reveille rattles recruits awake at 4:00 a.m. And they still march four miles a day to a loudly shouted cadence. But they exercise only four times a week and the pace is not at all grueling. Workouts start with fairly easy exercises lasting only 30 minutes, since most recruits aren't in particularly good shape when they arrive. This 'feminized' physical regimen is rationalized by 'sports science' people, who recommend a program that middle age to older citizens recognize as one that guarantees a minimum of injuries. In fact, the Navy admits[215] that "...*what exactly constitutes a 'fit' entry-level sailor has yet to be determined ... specialists have yet to nail down specific requirements.*"

This kinder, gentler boot camp is now starting to issue every recruit a special 'blues card' that goes in a shirt pocket. It is meant to remind homesick, scared, tired recruits that they're not alone. "*Help is only a question away,*" it says and it details who to talk with about depression and other problems.

The reason given for this 'feminization' of Navy boot camp is that it reduces the problem of 'sexual harassment' of female sailors by male sailors. Endless 'sensitivity training' classes and emphasis on rules of conduct between males and females are pervasive in boot camp. "*Rules are so strict that if a female recruit fell down in the snow in front of him, he would not help her until being granted permission by a commander,*" says a young male[216] recruit.

The Navy's nine-and-a-half-week boot camp is a time of military indoctrination, rigorous physical training and general preparation for assignment to a ship. But the old 'obstacle course,' a physically demanding test of strength and endurance, has been changed and renamed the 'confidence course.' This change is more than semantic. The physical requirements have been reduced for all -- including the traditional swimming tests. Why is this happening? Since shipboard sailors have not engaged in actual combat since the closing stages of World War II, the atmosphere aboard many ships is becoming more and more the same as civilian commercial enterprises. Sailors are no longer viewed as 'warriors' who may be called on to fight off kamikaze suicide attacks of a determined enemy or even the more realistic modern threat of attack by cruise missiles. Consequently, traditional warfighting standards are disappearing. If sailors are not expected to salute anyone aboard ship other than officers anymore, why should they be trained to salute in boot camp? If sailors no longer march in the fleet, why train them to march extensively in boot camp? Feminized standards of a 'caring' workplace are replacing the traditional Navy training programs.

Captain Whitehead, with a PhD in psychology, notes that some "...*old dinosaurs in the Navy...*" scoff at the more humane boot camp. She refers to male and female recruits as "...*the youngsters in our care.*" While all of the Navy's traditional trainers in the past cared a great deal about their charges (they took their role as *en loco parentis* very seriously), they understood that real 'caring' required that the recruits be trained to meet the wartime exigencies of battle. This meant rigorous physical and mental standards of conduct -- military discipline.

As an example of how these standards have been 'feminized,' listen to Kate O'Bierne, a member of the 1992 Presidential Commission on Women in

---

215 Ibid, pp. 13.
216 Ibid, Johnson, Dirk.

Combat. O'Bierne states[217] that "*A standard for shipboard performance was that two sailors be able to carry a 150-pound shipmate on a stretcher up a ladder and through a hatch to the deck above. This sensible requirement has been a staple of training since World War II when ships were attacked and set on fire. Sailors below decks were required to carry their shipmates topside where they had a chance to survive. Before women were assigned to ships, fully 100 percent of males were able to perform this task. But upon introducing females into ship crews, it was found that two females could not perform this task. Only 8 percent of females were able to meet this standard. So what was the answer?* **Change the standard.** Instead of requiring two persons, the new requirement would be to share the burden with four persons. In this way, females could meet the requirement at the 100 percent level.*

Evidently, recruits at Navy boot camp do not march extensively. Or if they do, this disciplinary exercise is quickly forgotten. A Marine second lieutenant reports his view of the current Navy boot camp training. He observes that[218] "...*Yelling and screaming [in Navy boot camp] are kept to a minimum in order to limit the stress level for recruits. Recruits no longer march with rifles, due in part to the fact that 'the weapons could too easily be made ready to fire,' Navy boot camp officials say.*" This young Marine officer further observes that "...*changes have come about to make Navy boot camp more like the fleet. Senior sailors and officers in the fleet probably won't yell at their juniors, and the odds of a sailor marching with a rifle 'in the fleet' are admittedly slim. Sailors will now be trained in a minimum-stress environment designed to prepare them for the 'real world' of the fleet Navy. These decisions have been based on a faulty premise: that the 'real world' of the fleet Navy is preparing its sailors to fight a war.*"

2nd LT Gilmore tells of a recent experience with 'the new' Navy while organizing a military presentation at a professional sporting event. Color guards from each of the five services were present, as were several hundred Marines and sailors who would take part in the half-time show. When organizing the event, the Navy officer in charge explained to Gilmore that[219] "...*the Navy personnel would not do anything during the half-time show that resembled marching.*" Sailors weren't very good at marching, he reasoned, because they just don't march very often. Gilmore was told that the Navy officers had released their personnel for participation contingent upon their not marching, "...*because they would look bad next to the Marines.*"

2nd LT Gilmore was willing to smile at that but his smile quickly faded when he was told that the Marines would also be expected to 'not march' onto the playing field. Further attempts were made by the Navy to 'simplify' the ceremony by having the members in the units face and salute as individuals, because having a commander of troops shout 'Right Face!' and 'Present Arms!' would 'confuse the sailors.' Obviously, the Navy not only had lowered its 'marching discipline' standards for naval personnel, but they now insisted on lowering these standards for the Marine Corps personnel as well, a service which takes pride in this disciplinary activity.

---

217 O'Beirne, Kate, "Culture Wars, Gender Wars and WAR Wars," Panel Discussion sponsored by The Independent Women's Forum, Washington, DC, 22 April 1997.
218 Gilmore, Clifford W., "Core values need military bearing to win wars," NAVY TIMES, 28 April 1997.
219 Ibid, Gilmore, Clifford W.

The proud Marine observed that "...*Over 1,000 personnel hours were squandered as the Navy's leadership contemplated ways to avoid creating stress for its sailors and scrambled to tone down the comparative professionalism of a fellow service.*" Obviously, the 'feminization' of Navy boot camp has spread to the entire enlisted body. And it is attempting to 'feminize' the ground combat arm of the Navy, the U.S. Marine Corps.

Finally, 2nd Lt Gilmore observes "...*I salute my brothers and sisters in arms who have chosen to serve with the Navy...But I pray for them as well...Being in the belly of a ship that has a hole punched in the hull, fires raging through the passageways and water flooding around them will probably make them feel crazy. But there will be no timeout to gather thought and regain composure ... The time will come when a weapon must be fired. If they are not trusted to carry a weapon, they will not be prepared to fight ... The time will come when they will be asked to stand for their nation as professionals at arms. Honor, courage and commitment are fine traits and outstanding core values. But they are worthless to our military unless they are taught in a warfighting context.*"

The Navy leadership should listen to this prescient young Marine. America must wake up and demand that Navy leadership meet its responsibilities -- to train its people to fight and win wars! They must have the discipline and physical and mental skills required to survive in a hostile seaborne environment. If the Navy does not see to it that America's sons are prepared for such a demanding environment, America's mothers and fathers will not encourage them to serve in the Navy. No mother or father would want their sons in a military service which cared so little for their precious progeny's survival skills.

In their weaker moments, the radical feminists inside the U.S. Navy admit that lowered standards for females have resulted in <u>lower standards for all</u>. CAPT Cornelia de Groot Whitehead, the Navy boot camp commander, writes in NEWSWEEK[220] that "...*you report that in theory, the <u>women's obstacle course</u> at boot camp <u>was made easier</u> and renamed the 'confidence course,' and that [this] double standard rankled men ... The course designed in 1994 with <u>identical standards</u> for men and women, was built to promote confidence in maritime challenges.*" Indeed, the lower standards in boot camp raise the 'self esteem' of women but at the expense of <u>reduced standards</u> for both men and women. The standards are now identical in their mediocrity -- all because of the 'feminization' of the Navy's boot camp.

The lowering of standards has even carried over into the swimming requirement in the Navy. Can you imagine sailors who cannot swim? Recently, the Navy found that many of its sailors could not survive[221] if they fell overboard from a ship at sea or accidentally found themselves in the water for some other reason. "*Sailors already in the fleet may face discharge if they can't swim well enough...*" How could this be? Sailors are supposed to have demonstrated a minimum of swimming proficiency in boot camp. But only recently has the Navy found that boot camp is not training sailors to swim up to a standard that ensures their survival in even the most minimal emergency situation. The Navy now says that "...*Sailors failing to qualify as swimmers in boot camp will be dropped from the service if they don't meet requirements after three weeks of remedial training. In addition, the minimum requirements will become tougher.*"

---

220 de G. Whitehead, Cory, CAPT USN, "No Double Standard," NEWSWEEK, pp. 18, 2 June 1997.
221 Burlage, John, "Sailors who sink are out," NAVY TIMES, 21 April 1997.

The current rules require that to make swimmer third class, sailors now must only be able to "...*enter the water feet first from a minimum of five feet, swim 50 yards using any stroke and remain afloat for five minutes.*" Under new rules, recently invoked because of a concern that 'sailors who cannot swim, cannot survive,' require that a Navy recruit,
- Enter the water feet first from at least five feet
- Swim 50 yards using any 'survival stroke.' These are defined as the American crawl, or breast, side and back stroke
- Remain afloat for five minutes
- Enter the water feet first wearing a shirt and trousers
- Inflate the shirt by slowing air into it, then remove the trousers and inflate them for support
- Remain afloat until told to get out of the pool.

But these 'new rules' are only the traditional swimming requirements that have served the 'old Navy' well over the past 50 years. They were invoked, partially, from practical survival experience in World War II.

For example[222], the light cruiser Juneau was torpedoed off Guadalcanal, broke in two, and went down in 20 seconds. But as many as 100 members of her 700-man crew were hurled into the water and managed to inflate three life rafts. For a week, the seamen drifted and died; victims of exposure, thirst, delirium, and savage shark attacks. Some reached a small island but when help finally came, there were only ten men alive. They lived only by their ability to survive in the water. Thus, the Navy's traditional high standards of endurance swimming proficiency have been a part of boot camp sea-survival training for decades. Incredibly, these proven sea-survival standards have been weakened in the new 'feminized' Navy in the name of 'self esteem' and making naval careers 'female friendly.'

Indeed, the recent 'feminization' of the Navy has reduced swimming standards to such a level that even today's politically correct Navy realizes the survival vulnerability that it is imposing on sailors who 'cannot swim' but who are serving on ships where 'man overboard' is a real daily hazard of life. Standards have, indeed, been lowered in nearly every aspect of Navy life.

The 'Feminization' of the U.S. Navy Reduces Standards For All

So there you have it. From the Navy's prime source of officer candidates, the U.S. Naval Academy, to advanced jet aviation training, to enlisted sailors' boot camp, the standards are being lowered across the board to accommodate members of preferred groups who are 'not of the highest caliber.' Indeed, 'affirmative action' gone awry is the Navy's systemic problem. The 'feminization' of the entire Navy is the last straw in the chaotic disintegration of that great institution. In time, 'feminization' will also be the systemic problem for the nation's entire military establishment. This will lead to reduced standards for politically 'protected' groups, women and minorities, which in time produce reduced standards for all, including white males.

It is clear that the U.S. Navy has been slowly and subtly but determinedly lowering standards over time at the Navy's premiere source of naval officers, the U.S. Naval Academy. This pattern has pervaded every nook and cranny of standards in the U.S. Navy. From the Secretary of the

---

222 McFadden, Robert D., "Remembering the Juneau: New Navy Destroyer Honors Victims of Disaster at Sea," The New York Times, 20 April 1997.

Navy to the Chief of Naval Operations to naval officer recruitment, selection, and promotion to basic and advanced naval aviation training to Fleet Replacement Squadron training for minority and female aviation candidates to boot camp for enlisted personnel.

Consequently, we see **suicide** at the highest level of Navy leadership. We see **attrition rates** for females and minorities up to four times that of white males in advanced jet aviation training. We see fleet-wide safety-of-flight 'stand downs' for <u>unexplainable</u> causes. We see an **epidemic** of Field Naval Aviation Evaluation Boards (FNAEBs) for substandard carrier pilots in fleet operational squadrons. We see **drug and car-theft rings** at the Naval Academy. We see sailors who cannot swim. All **unexplainable.   Baloney!**

Conclusion and Summary

Judge Robert H. Bork, a conservative Republican, describes[223] an America 'Slouching Towards Gomorrah.' He is quite pessimistic about America's decline; morally, educationally, legally, and in our military institutions. He writes that "...*[our predecessors] can hardly have had any conception of just how thoroughly things would fall apart as the center failed to hold in the last third of this century. [They could] hardly have foreseen that passionate intensity, uncoupled from morality, would shred the fabric of Western culture.*"

Samuel P. Huntington, the renowned scholar and national security advisor in the Carter administration, places Judge Bork's view in a higher historical plane, that of the clash of 'civilizations.' He observes that[224] "*History ends at least once and occasionally more often in the history of every civilization. As the civilization's <u>universal state</u>[225] emerges, its people become blinded by what Toynbee called the '<u>mirage of immortality</u>' and convinced that theirs is the final form of human society.*" He further observes that "*The citizens of such universal states, 'in defiance of apparently plain facts,' are prone to regard it ... as the Promised Land, the goal of human endeavors.*" History has shown, however, that such societies (those who have beaten their chests and exclaimed '*We are the world's sole remaining <u>superpower</u>*') are usually societies whose history is about to decline.

The moral, civil, and societal decay of a civilization leads to the stage of invasion[226] "*...when the civilization, no longer <u>able</u> to defend itself because it is no longer <u>willing</u> to defend itself, lies wide open to **barbarian** invaders, who often come from another, younger, more powerful*

---

[223] Bork, Robert H., "Slouching Towards Gomorrah: Modern Liberalism and American Decline," HarperCollins, 1996.
[224] Huntington, Samuel P., "The Clash of Civilizations and the Remaking of World Order," pp. 301, Simon & Schuster, 1996.
[225] Toynbee, Arnold, "A Study of History," pp. 244, Abridgement of Volumes I-VI, by D.C. Somervell, Oxford University Press, 1946, Fourteenth printing 1958. Toynbee observes that the '<u>universal state</u>' occurs when '*a disintegrating civilization purchases a reprieve by submitting to a forcible political unification ... the classic example is the Roman Empire into which the Hellenic Society was forcibly gathered up in the penultimate chapter of its history.*'
[226] Ibid, Huntington, Samuel P., pp. 303.

civilization." Obviously, a civilization without its most effective and strongest possible military cannot prevail over future 'barbarian' invaders.

How does this apply to the United States of America, the strongest and most dominant component of Western Civilization? Huntington observes that 'multiculturalism' is the most dangerous challenge to our future.[227] "*A more immediate and dangerous challenge exists in the United States. Historically, American national identity has been defined culturally by the heritage of Western Civilization and politically by the principles of the* **American Creed** *on which Americans overwhelmingly agree: liberty, democracy, individualism, equality before the law, constitutionalism, and private property.*" He, among others, has observed that a force has risen on the plain -- multiculturalism -- that, if unchecked, will accelerate the decline of American civilization.

"*In the late twentieth century ... American identity has come under concentrated and sustained onslaught from a small but influential number of intellectuals and publicists. In the name of* multiculturalism *they have denounced ... the 'systematic bias toward European culture and its derivatives' in education and 'the dominance of the European-American monocultural perspective.*" Huntington further observes that "*In the name of multiculturalism they have attacked the identification of the United States with Western civilization, denied the existence of a common American culture, and promoted racial, ethnic, and other subnational cultural identities and groupings.*" In the context of this book, one must identify the radical feminists as the modern liberals who would add 'gender' to this cultural identity and grouping.

Huntington quotes Arthur M. Schlesinger, Jr., who says "*The multiculturalists are very often ethnocentric separatists who see little in the Western heritage other than Western crimes.*" The radical feminists are in this menagerie, claiming 'sexism' and dominance of 'dead-white-males' as the ultimate disgrace of Western Civilization.

Huntington reminds us that[228] "*The leaders of other countries have ... at times attempted to disavow their cultural heritage and shift the identity of their country from one civilization to another. In no case to date have they succeeded and they have instead created schizophrenic torn countries. The American* multiculturalists *similarly reject their country's cultural heritage. Instead of attempting to identify the United States with another civilization, however, they wish to create a country of many civilizations, which is to say a country not belonging to any civilization and lacking a cultural core. History shows that no country so constituted can long endure as a coherent society. A mulicivilizational United States will not be the United States; it will be the United Nations.*" And with this identity, we will be swept into the dust bin of history.

With incisive insight, Huntington tells us that[229] "*The* multiculturalists *also challenged a central element of the* **American Creed**, *by substituting for the rights of individuals the rights of groups, defined largely in terms of race, ethnicity,* **sex**, *and sexual preference. The Creed Gunnar Myrdal said in the 1940s, reinforcing the comments of foreign observers dating from Hector St. John de Crevecoeur and Alexis de Tocqueville, has been* **'the cement in the structure of this great and**

---

227 Ibid, Huntington, Samuel P., pp. 305.
228 Ibid, Huntington, Samuel P., pp. 306.
229 Ibid, Huntington, Samuel P., pp. 306.

disparate nation.' 'It has been our fate as a nation,' Richard Hofstader agreed, *'not to have ideologies but to be one.'"* The radical feminists and their allies in the Clinton administration, Congress, and in the American populace walk away from these basic tenets at their peril. If we allow this betrayal, we do so at the peril of **all**!

Huntington poses a post-Cold-War world as one in which ideologies no longer dominate in conflicts but where civilizations clash as a result of *fault-line wars* such as Bosnia, the Middle East, Azerbaijan, and in time Southeast Asia. In this context, he observes that "*In an era in which peoples everywhere define themselves in cultural terms, what place is there for a society without a cultural core and defined only by a political creed? In a multicivizational world where culture counts, the United States could be simply the last anomalous holdover from a fading Western world where ideology counted. Rejection of the* **Creed** *and of Western civilization means* **the end of the United States of America** *as we have known it. It also means effectively* **the end of Western civilization**."

Huntington believes[230] that the clash between the multiculturalists and the defenders of Western civilization and the **American Creed** is '*the real clash within the American segment of Western civilization*." He is absolutely correct. Multiculturalism, the most virulent and damaging component of <u>modern liberalism</u> has the potential to destroy the United States of America. Others have identified this common enemy.

Judge Bork identifies[231] the defining characteristics of <u>modern liberalism</u> as "...'radical egalitarianism' (the equality of outcomes rather than of opportunities) and 'radical individualism' (the drastic reduction of limits to person gratification)..." He identifies 'radical feminism' as the "...*most destructive and fanatical*..." element of this liberalism. He further describes radical feminism as "... *totalitarian in spirit*." He characterizes it as a Neo-Marxist movement which has an agenda aimed at utterly destroying America's prized institutions.

The Author, in his recent book, "The New Totalitarians: Bosnia as a Mirror of America's Future," describes this 'totalitarian spirit' in minute detail, especially as it manifests itself in the chaotic disintegration of the U.S. Navy -- a prized American institution which is being destroyed by a radical feminist agenda. The feminization of the U.S. military is occurring under a coordinated 'social engineering' agenda that would serve as a model for a New American Civilization -- one that would destroy the traditional family, be hostile to traditional religion, and attempt to 'remake' human beings through the use of **'thought control'** -- right out of Stalin's Soviet totalitarian handbook.

The U.S. Navy is in the middle stages of a chaotic disintegration. This collapse is widespread and total -- from the suicide of the former Chief of Naval Operations to the complete breakdown of trust in naval aviation to the existence of drug and car-theft rings at the U.S. Naval Academy to sailors who cannot swim and who cannot carry an injured shipmate topside in a burning, sinking combatant ship.

The chaotic disintegration of a human being, ADM Jeremy Boorda, is a metaphor for the concomitant disintegration of naval aviation. The chaotic disintegration of naval aviation is, in turn, a metaphor for the larger American civilization. The naval metaphors are of interest because their outcomes are 'collapsed in time.' The ramp of an aircraft carrier is an

---

230 Ibid, Huntington, Samuel P., pp. 307.
231 Ibid, Bork, Robert H.

equal opportunity killer. The results of reduced standards and a complete breakdown of trust are more quickly apparent in the naval metaphors than they are in the more gradual disintegration of American civilization from within. But both collapses are the result of similar complex non-linear factors.

The U.S. Navy is sinking under a radical feminist assault. What the Japanese could not accomplish at Pearl Harbor and what the tyrannical forces of Soviet communism could not accomplish during the Cold War is being accomplished by America's radical feminists and their allies in the Executive Branch and in Congress with support from the nation's mass media. The U.S. Navy is being torpedoed by the very government it serves. While the American people sleep!

Bill Lind, a military historian and TV personality, describes radical feminism[232] as "...*Marxism translated from economics to culture.*" Lind further recognizes that[233] "...*placing women in the military is potentially more disruptive than allowing openly homosexual males there...*" This statement was based on his study of the Frankfurt School, a group of Marxist intellectuals who, following World War I, worked to transfer Marxism from economics to culture. In addition, Friedrich Engels[234], the German socialist, quite early-on, suggested using radical feminism to break down the Western capitalist economic system.

The New Totalitarians, including the radical feminists as their most dangerous element, intend the destruction of every American institution constructed over the past 200-plus years and strengthened by the noble, sacrificing G.I. generation -- including the U.S. military. Indeed, these **'barbarians**[235]**'** have nearly destroyed the U.S. Navy. They have invoked underground 'affirmative action' programs for women and minorities which have reduced standards across-the-board. And when the resulting inevitable failures become recognizable to patriotic naval personnel who would 'report' those failures to the American people, the New Totalitarians -- the barbarians, the radical feminists and their allies -- implemented a **campaign of terror** to intimidate these loyal American patriots.

This **intimidation** by **terror** reaches (in some degree or other) from the highest levels of the Navy to officer promotions at all levels, to naval aviation training to the U.S. Naval Academy and, finally, to the so-called

---

232 Lind, Bill, "The Next Revolution," NET-TV, 10:00 p.m., 30 October 1996.
233 Lind, Bill, "Political Correctness in the Military," 'Modern War,' NET-TV, 8:00 p.m., 6 December 1996.
234 Friedrich Engels (1820-1895) was the German socialist who, in the mid-1800s, collaborated with Karl Marx (1818-1883) to develop Marxist economic theory.
235 Ibid, Bork, Robert H., pp. 313, 342. Bork reminds us that "...*We are entering a period of tribal hostilities . . . we may expect . . . a rise in interethnic violence, a slowing of economic productivity, a vulgarization of scholarship (which is already well under way), and increasing government intrusion into our lives in the name of producing greater equality and ethnic peace, which will, predictably, produce still greater polarization and fractiousness . . .* " Bork further relates **radical feminism** to **barbarism**. Quoting Ortega y Gasset, he observes ". . . *'Civilization is before all, the will to live in common . . . Barbarism is the tendency to disassociation. Accordingly, all barbarous epochs have been times of human scattering, of the pullation of tiny groups, separate from and hostile to one another.'* Bork's final conclusion, *"**Multiculturalism is barbarism**, and it is bringing us to a <u>barbarous epoch</u>."*

civilian 'free' press. This **reign of terror** must not continue. If Americans allow it to succeed with the U.S. Navy, then the U.S. Army and then the entire U.S. military, all will be lost. For that which is now being visited on the U.S. Navy will be visited on all of American civilization in time. In fact, it already is being visited[236,237] on us to some degree -- in our public schools, our universities, our work places, our public air waves, our neighborhoods, our churches, our justice system, and our families. The only major difference between the chaotic disintegration of the U.S. Navy and that of American civilization is <u>time</u>. The collapse is already occurring in the Navy. The seeds of disintegration have slowly been planted[238] in American civilization over the past thirty years. It may be too late to remove the destructive weeds from the U.S. Navy. It is not too late to destroy those seeds planted by the New Totalitarians -- the **barbarians** -- in American civilization. Wake up America! Before it is too late!

The United States of America is at a crossroads in its experiment with democracy. Danger, as described here, lurks. We must not be foolish enough to believe that we are immune from these dangers. For, as the distinguished scholar, Will Durant, observed in his ten-volume account of 'The Story of Civilization,' all civilizations work against a common enemy. The enemy is the **barbarian**[239], reincarnated today as the multiculturalist, the radical feminist;

> *"For **barbarism**[240] is always around civilization, <u>amid it</u> and beneath it, ready to engulf it by arms, or mass migration, or unchecked fertility. **Barbarism** is like the jungle; it never admits its defeat; it waits patiently for centuries to recover the territory it has lost."*

---

236   Atkinson, Gerald L., "The New Totalitarians: Bosnia as a Mirror of America's Future," Atkinson Associates Press, 1996.
237   Ibid, Bork, Robert H.
238   Ibid, Atkinson, Gerald L.
239   Durant, Will, "The Story of Civilization: Our Oriental Heritage, Volume 1", pp. 265, Simon and Schuster, 1935 & 1963.
240   Judge Bork concludes his book with a quote from Ortega y Gasset. *"Barbarism is a tendency to disassociation. Accordingly, all barbarous epochs have been times of human scattering, of the pullation of tiny groups, <u>separate from</u> and <u>hostile to one another</u>."* Bork concludes this definition of barbarism with the observation, *"Multiculturalism is barbarism, and it is bringing us to a barbarous epoch."* Ibid, Bork, Robert H., pp. 313, 342.

Index

A

The Actors 3
  The Author 3, 31, 33, 35, 39, 62, 76, 84, 89
  The Flight Instructors 3, 9, 18, 27, 28, 29, 30, 32, 33, 56
  The Flight Surgeon(s) 3, 15
  The Lawyers 3, 11, 25
  The Newspaper 3, 25, 32
  The Relative 3, 31
  The Reporter 24, 25, 26, 30, 32
  The Student Pilot 3, 6, 9, 10, 11, 12, 13, 14, 18, 19, 20, 21, 24, 25, 28, 30, 32, 55, 56, 65
    carrier qualification grades 13
    unsatisfactory performance 13
    personal problems 14
  The Wing Commander 3, 6, 12, 14, 16, 20, 21, 24, 30, 31, 56, 65
    bullet-proof 29
ADM Jeremy Boorda 25, 33, 60, 98
ADM Stanley Arthur 25, 42, 60
Admiral's Mast 21
affirmative action 1, 6, 19, 43, 44, 45, 47, 49, 55, 56, 57, 64, 68, 85, 95
  quotas 21
airsick 35, 79
American civilization 100
American Creed 97
Army Secretary Togo West 87
attrition rates 52, 96

B

barbarian 96, 99, 100
basic standard of fairness 28
Blue Angels 57
  affirmative action pressures on 58
boot camp 91
  CAPT Cornelia de Groot Whitehead 91
  CDR Xzana Tellis 91
  confidence course 93
  feminization of 92
  kinder, gentler 92
  lower standards for all 94
  sailors who cannot swim 94
  survive in the water 95

C

CAPT Charles W. Nesby 40, 45
CAPT Herb Ladley, USN (Ret.) 77
CAPT Kenneth 'Dutch' Rauch, USN (Retired) 45
carrier qualification (CQ) 13
chaotic disintegration 2
Chief of Naval Air Training (CNATRA) 6
  CNATRA 3, 16, 20, 21, 26, 27, 28, 65
Chief of Naval Education and Training (CNET) 23
Chief of Naval Operations (CNO) 25, 98
Clinton administration 26, 63, 70, 75
COL Kelly Hamilton 89
Commanding Officer (CO) 10
common enemy 100
complete absence of standards 21
Congress 2, 26, 75, 99
cover-up 2

D

DACOWITS 87
discrimination 40
double standards 5, 28, 31, 32, 35
downs 6, 10, 12, 13, 16
  excused 11, 16, 20

F

failure rates 50
feminization 33, 71, 85
Field Naval Aviation Evaluation Boards 54
  epidemic of 96
  FNAEBs 54, 57
Fleet Replacement Squadron (FRS) 3, 15, 34
flight familiarization (FAM) 10
  below average grades in 13
fornicating 71
  aboard the aircraft carrier USS Nimitz 71
fraternization 2, 10, 25, 27, 28
Freedom of Information Act (FOIA) 25

G

grounded 12, 14, 16, 19

H

helicopter 28

I

incident (accident) rates 53
Inspector General (IG) investigation 22
  formal IG investigation 23

IG investigation report 26
informal IG investigation 23
instructor pilots (IPs) 9

J

Jerry R. Cadick 84

L

landing signal officer (LSO) 14, 33
LCDR Stacy Bates 35
Lemoore 15
Lewis Puller, Jr. 73
LT Carey Dunai Lohrenz 46, 78
LT Gerald DiLeonardo 55
LT Kara Hultgreen 26, 33, 60, 77
LT Rebecca Hansen 25, 60
LT Shannon Workman 55, 62
Ltjg Gary Commock 40

M

Marine Captain 9, 12
maritime pipeline 17
mass media 5, 60, 99
    Bill Press 76
    Bonnie Erbe 75
    Cokie Roberts 72
    Eleanor Clift 75
    Elizabeth Farnsworth 72
    Evan Thomas 76
    George C. Wilson 62
    Georgie Anne Geyer 61
    Richard Cohen 72
modern liberals 97
morale 2
multiculturalism 33, 70, 97

N

Naval Aviation Medical Institute NAMI 14, 16
Naval Aviation Safety Center 14
naval flight officers (NFOs) 35
naval metaphors 98
night carrier landings 63

O

obsession 7, 16
officer promotion 26

P

pregnancy and parenthood 71
preliminary investigation (PI) 11
President Clinton 72, 73
Progress Review Board (PRB)
    PRB 13
    Progress Review Board 5, 10, 12, 16
protector of the trust 1
psychiatric evaluation 16

Q

quotas 45

R

radar intercept officer (RIO) 33
radical feminist propaganda 60
radical feminists 2, 43, 51, 64, 80, 87
RADM Lyle G. Bien 47
RADM William B. Hayden 44, 55
reduced minimum qualification standards 54
reduced qualification/training standards 33, 94
reduced standards
    damning evidence of 56
remedial courses 46
romantic liaison 9

S

safety of flight 20
sailors who cannot swim 98
sexual harassment 11
Sgt Maj Harold Overstreet 86
social engineering 43, 70
stick forces 83
stick-force-per-g 83
suicide 15

T

Tailhook 5, 19
terror 1, 6, 29
    abject fear 29
    campaign of 4, 5, 25, 32, 65, 99
    cold edge of 12
    intimidation and fear 19
    reign of 6, 30, 32, 33, 72, 100
    reign of terror 3
    scapegoated and terrorized 6
    shivers of 69
the dark side 29
thought control 69, 98
    sensitivity training 69, 70
ticket-punching careerists 87
totalitarianism 69
trust 1
    bond of 28
    breakdown of 1, 5, 65, 98
    is being destroyed 59
    loss of 58
    pyramid of 59
Tuskegee Airmen 36
    attrition rate 37
    Black pride 37
    training/qualification standards 38
    mutual trust 38

U

U.S. Air Force 5
U.S. Army 2, 70
U.S. military 70, 100
U.S. Naval Academy 5, 33, 46, 60, 66, 67
   breakdown of trust at 61
   cheating scandal 66
   lowered academic standards at 61, 89
   review panel 68
   terror at 66
U.S. Navy
   chaotic disintegration 98
   radical feminist assault 99
   stand downs 85, 96
U.S. Navy's
   systemic problem 68
uncommon self-control 79
Uniform Code of Military Justice 9, 30
USS Abraham Lincoln 33, 47
USS Eisenhower 46, 62

V

veterans 72, 75
Vietnam War 73

W

WANDAS 20, 25, 56
warrior 1, 2, 4, 31, 32, 61, 69, 81, 86, 87, 88, 93
White House staff 74, 75
wings of gold 4, 35, 52
women-in-combat 32, 59
   aerobic capacity 81
   high-technology 88
   physical strength 82
   strength, stamina, and endurance 83, 84, 85, 87